NAVIGATING YOUR CAREER

Five steps to success
in the new world of work

KERRY DAWKINS

GRAEME CODRINGTON

PENGUIN BOOKS

Published by the Penguin Group
Penguin Books (South Africa) (Pty) Ltd, Block D, Rosebank Office Park,
181 Jan Smuts Avenue, Parktown North, Johannesburg, 2196, South Africa
Penguin Group (USA) Inc, 375 Hudson Street, New York, New York 10014, USA
Penguin Group (Canada), 90 Eglinton Avenue East, Suite 700, Toronto, Ontario, Canada
M4P 2Y3 (a division of Pearson Penguin Canada Inc)
Penguin Books Ltd, 80 Strand, London WC2R 0RL, England
Penguin Ireland, 25 St Stephen's Green, Dublin 2,
Ireland (a division of Penguin Books Ltd)
Penguin Group (Australia), 250 Camberwell Road, Camberwell, Victoria 3124, Australia
(a division of Pearson Australia Group Pty Ltd)
Penguin Books India Pvt Ltd, 11 Community Centre,
Panchsheel Park, New Delhi – 110 017, India
Penguin Group (NZ), 67 Apollo Drive, Mairangi Bay, Auckland 1310, New Zealand
(a division of Pearson New Zealand Ltd)

Penguin Books (South Africa) (Pty) Ltd, Registered Offices:
Block D, Rosebank Office Park, 181 Jan Smuts Avenue, Parktown North,
Johannesburg, 2196, South Africa

www.penguinbooks.co.za

First published by Penguin Books (South Africa) (Pty) Ltd 2012
Reprinted 2012

Copyright © Kerry Dawkins and Graeme Codrington 2012

ISBN 978-0-14-353026-8

Cover by Flame Design
Printed and bound by Interpak Books, Pietermaritzburg

FSC
www.fsc.org
FSC° C105736

The mark of
responsible forestry

Kerry:
For my team, Jonathan, Daniella, Matt, Ben and Margie.
Thank you for the space and time to navigate my career and
support others in their career navigation.

Graeme:
For my wife, Jane, and daughters, Amy, Hannah and Rebecca.
You are my reason to get up and go to work every day.

CONTENTS

DEVELOP THE POWER
TO NAVIGATE YOUR CAREER

Your career is not a hobby. It's non-negotiable really: you *need* to succeed in your career. You have to pay for the house, the cars, the children's education, your next holiday and whatever other lifestyle choices you have made. Like most people, your career is your only ticket to any form of financial success in life. A few people find that building a career is easy. For most people, though, it's tough.

Your boss mentioned a divisional restructuring. You have no idea what you would do if you were forced to find a new job. The talk, arranged by HR, about the new world of work didn't do anything to alleviate that stress about the long term. In fact, it just left you feeling scared and suspicious.

That reminds you that you had better set up that LinkedIn account like Mike suggested. Your friends are going on holidays to the coast and you have promised the family that they can do the same. You just can't admit right now to the others – or to your family – that cash is a little tight. And the car needs fixing too. Hopefully it can wait just a few months more.

And then there are the demands on you and your time. Family activities you need to attend and friends who need your help. If you could just sleep properly and not feel so tired all the time, that would help.

Yes, managing your career – and your life – can be tough indeed. You wonder how some lucky people get to do work that they really like. You always dreamt of that for yourself, but right now there seems to be no chance of doing what you truly want. You have too many bills to pay so you must just keep doing what you're doing now.

And just like that, you fall into The Trap.

THE TRAP

When you are faced with a career dilemma, you may attempt to solve it by speaking to a couple of people or by posting your resumé online, hoping that someone will come calling with that perfect job. When that doesn't work, you give up and convince yourself that you are lucky to have your current job and that only especially blessed people get to do what they love. You may even enter that 'waiting area', where you wait to be happy, wait for the perfect moment, wait to have enough money.

This is The Trap: thinking that some time in the future you'll have the time, the energy, the resources, the network, the skills, the lucky break, or some other opportunity you somehow can't access now. And so you try to survive your current situation. Waiting.

Most people are better at coping than at taking control and making choices that powerfully propel them forward to success. Have you noticed the increasing evidence of people's 'just coping' in our society? The excessive and increasing use of prescription drugs to reduce and manage stress; excessive drinking to drown the sorrows of the week; job-hopping for small increases in pay; lack of engagement in the workplace; lack of energy amongst workers; poor service; incomplete work, and more. Companies now have to provide incentives and awards to encourage people just to complete the work they were hired for and are being paid to do. These are people who are treading water in their careers. Just waiting.

This may feel like your only option, or even seem like a good tactic, except for the fact that career dilemmas can be – and have been – resolved by many people in many different situations. Many people have escaped The Trap. There are actual people out there who, instead of accepting that work is something that just pays the bills, have found or created work that pays the bills *and* is fulfilling and, in many cases, also positively impacts the world.

When it comes to overcoming career dilemmas, what most people lack is not the competence to do the work (current or new) but rather the skill to navigate their careers effectively. On their own and with their current level of skill, it is rare for people to come up with the ideas and options they need to escape The Trap and overcome career dilemmas. They remain caught in The Trap by seeking quick-fix solutions based on the latest popular trends or suggestions from well-meaning but poorly informed family and friends.

What they need are the skills and attitudes that will propel them to career success. This is possible for everyone. This is what this book is all about.

TAKING RESPONSIBILITY

Most people typically don't think of themselves as 'career navigators' as they're too focused on the job they're currently doing and they fail to see the impact that their careers have on themselves and their communities. If they did, they would invest much more energy in looking for new and better ways to enhance their career navigation strategies and skills. Any time they tried to find jobs and failed, they'd stop to try a new strategy. Any time they were declined raises or promotions, they'd try something new or carve new roles for themselves. Any time they came home drained and disillusioned, they'd seek out something new, or at least place another marker on the career navigation journey.

Many people cause themselves a great deal of grief by not realising that it's their duty to become good at navigating their careers. Instead of moaning, complaining, becoming despondent and finding ways to cope, they need to focus on improving career navigation skills and strategies.

This is why we wrote this book. We are of the opinion that almost all career dilemmas can be overcome by simply thinking and behaving differently. To free themselves from The Trap, people need to take responsibility for their careers; go about creating their own realities and powerfully choose the options that will allow them to be their best.

In this book, instead of seeking quick-fix strategies, we explore the mindsets that successful career navigators use every day to secure opportunities in the new world of work and become their best. This is something you can start today and do every day for the rest of your life.

SEEKING YOUR ANSWER

There are people who have used these strategies to create fulfilling lives. They will not compromise; they persevere to find the answers that work for them. They seek and find answers to questions like:

- What work would make me jump out of bed each morning?
- What role do I need to play to have energy to do my best?
- What will allow me to bring everything I have to my work?
- What do I require in a job to be engaged?
- How does my job impact the world?
- How can I be powerfully in action?

They find what inspires them to use their discretionary energy to pursue a goal. That gives them the strength to fight like heroes and sacrifice their comforts for the greater good. That's what inspires them to powerful action and excellence. That's what makes them *be* their best.

THERE IS HOPE

In a world filled with those content in jobs that increase their stress levels and drain their energy, there are those people who know exactly what it is to navigate their careers – and make a difference to the world along the way.

When we interviewed successful career navigators for this book, it was clear that their success was not due to luck, but rather the result of careful and persistent effort to become the people they wanted to be and have the impact they set out to achieve.

Both of us, authors of this book, feel successful in our own career navigation. The lessons we have set out to share in this book include our own experiences; the insights of key successful people we have interviewed, and the results of years of research and career counselling with many hundreds of people whom we have successfully taught the navigation skills required for career success.

The purpose of this book is to share the mindsets and strategies routinely employed by the best career navigators. We hope to raise your awareness of your own *unconscious incompetence* in career navigation. This is a crucial first step towards obtaining and applying the necessary skills for effective career navigation. It's the beginning of the road and, through the use and practice of the tools we'll explore, our hope is that you'll arrive at *conscious competence* and be able to navigate your career effectively.

Above all, we hope that the advice in this book will help you to find a job that you love, that you're excited about doing and that fulfils you at the deepest level.

THE STRUCTURE OF THE BOOK

In Chapter 1, we explore career dilemmas in more detail and introduce you to six real-life people and their career dilemmas. In Chapter 2, we present and explain our five-stage Career Navigation Model and the mindsets that we suggest you adopt for successful career navigation. Chapters 3 to 7 cover each stage of the Career Navigation Model in more detail. In Chapter 8, we discuss common career challenges.

We also suggest exercises throughout the book. At the end of each chapter, there is a coaching section, where we provide a number of exercises you can do on your own or with friends who can help you to develop yourself. We know that you may just want to read the book but we hope you'll take the time to pause and complete the exercises. They are part of how you will develop your career navigation skills. Just reading this book is not going to help you navigate your career. Career navigation is something you have to *do*, not just something to think about.

THE AUTHORS

Kerry Dawkins is a career development specialist and through Potential at Work (www.patwork.co.za), she provides mentoring services to all levels of employees, assisting them with overcoming career dilemmas. Kerry holds a Master's in business administration as well as two other degrees. Kerry is the careers expert for both Career Junction and *SA Careers Focus*, a South African careers magazine. In these positions, she has been exposed to the rising number of career dilemmas and, in an effort to spread the necessary skills and mindsets to escape The Trap, she created the process of Navigating Your Career (together with learner and facilitator resources). She has established the Association of Career Coaches and Advisors, which seeks to educate and support South African career advisors and coaches.

It seemed a natural fit for Kerry to collaborate with **Graeme Codrington** in writing this book, as he is a recognised international expert on the new world of work. Graeme runs his own strategy consulting company, TomorrowToday (www.tomorrowtoday.biz) with bases in London, Johannesburg, Toronto and Singapore. He is a well-known futurist, speaker and board advisor on issues relating to the future and our changing world. Graeme has a Doctorate in business administration as well as four other degrees, and is guest faculty with three of the world's leading business schools (Duke, London and GIBS). He has authored three other books, all published by Penguin Books, including the bestselling *Mind the Gap* (updated 2011) and *Future-proof Your Child* (2008).

1

CAREER DILEMMAS

'For the past 33 years, I have looked in the mirror every morning and asked myself: "If today were the last day of my life, would I want to do what I am about to do today?" And whenever the answer has been "No" for too many days in a row, I know I need to change something.'
Steve Jobs, Stanford University commencement address, 12 June 2005

There are very few people who jump out of bed every morning, excited and delighted at the prospect of the work they'll do in the day ahead. Even fewer people have a deep sense of calm assurance that they'll be able to keep doing so for the rest of their lives. Most people experience this feeling only occasionally and it is normally erased from their memories by the end of the first meeting at the office that day.

It's all too easy to think that those few people who find their work genuinely fulfilling and enriching are lucky or that they had some special help along the way, like being rich, or clever, or part of a well-connected family. The reality is that smart, rich people are as likely to be unhappy in their jobs as anyone else. In fact, research has shown that beyond an average income of US$80 000, there is no noticeable increase in happiness resulting from higher earnings.

So if money doesn't buy happiness, what does? The key to a fulfilling life at work is simply learning the skills and mindsets required to *navigate your career*.

This is not just a cute catchphrase. The days when your best career advice was to 'get a good job in a big company and stay there' are long gone. The average worker now changes jobs every few years and is likely to change careers as many as five times before retirement. And retirement itself may soon be a thing of the past. The truth is that very few people have been taught how to craft a career path. People are taught how to do their jobs, but not how to move between them or to navigate within them. People learn how to handle different work environments, but not how to craft the ones they actually want and that would serve them best.

In larger organisations, it used to be possible to rely on the human resources department to manage your career for you, provided you were okay with someone else being in the driving seat. But that hasn't been true for many years now, both because HR no longer think that's their role and, frankly, because people want more control over their own lives. As before, some people get stuck because incompetent – or malicious – bosses block their career advancement. Some discover that the choices they made do not lead to the jobs they were hoping for. Others are just unlucky: their companies are acquired, their teams downsized or redeployed; or maybe their jobs change as the world changes around them. Whatever the reason, too many people feel they are stuck in their current positions, and are not entirely sure of what to do next. And no one is volunteering to show them the way.

A WORLD OF POSSIBILITIES

The current world of work offers a vast array of career options and job possibilities. The increasing prevalence of more flexible work arrangements, individualised workplace experiences, multinational teams and corporate lattices (which have replaced corporate ladders) are all expected to increase these options further. In this environment, it is more important than ever to learn the skills and mindsets required to navigate your career.

This increased choice and complexity may cause you to become confused about what new steps to take in your career, which job option to choose, and how to find or create meaningful work. A person facing any of these troubles may feel overwhelmed, fearful, indecisive or despairing. These problems, relating to a person's career and workplace, are what we call *career dilemmas*.

Kerry and her team have spent many years helping people to identify and solve these career dilemmas. Some have been students looking for their first jobs, but most have been people already working or people between jobs. This is the focus of this book. Kerry's team at Potential at Work help people through five important stages of responding to a career dilemma. Unfortunately, there are no easy solutions.

We've worked with hundreds of people and one thing is clear: being deliberate with your career and following the necessary steps, which we'll share in this book, will get you the results you are looking for.

This book includes some of their success stories, not only as inspiration for you, but also to help you see our process in action. As you read their stories, you'll notice how their thinking and, subsequently, their career decisions have evolved as they learnt more about our process. Over the last 20 years, as we've worked with more and more people, we've learnt what works best and, perhaps more importantly, what does not work or even causes career damage. We're delighted to share with you both our own experience and the trials and triumphs of our many friends and clients. We expect that, if you follow the advice we have collected in this book, you will soon join the ranks of people who simply love what they do and live to do it.

SIX PEOPLE, SIX STORIES: SHARED CAREER DILEMMAS

To get a glimpse of the difficulties of navigating a career, we now introduce you to six people. They're real people, although we've changed names and details for this book. We've met many people like them and you probably have too. You may feel like you recognise them or it may even feel like you're looking in the mirror. As you read their profiles, look for the issues and concepts that match your situation – and then watch as their stories unfold through this book. These stories will help to explain our five-stage method. Over the years, we've found that, even for very diverse people in very different situations, the causes of career dilemmas and their solutions are limited to a small number of common elements.

Philip

Philip was a 40-year-old financial manager in a large corporate company when he was passed over for a promotion. Looking tired and deflated when we met him, he said, 'They just don't get it. They have employed a new guy to take the role I should have been given. I think they will head into serious problems if they promote people with so little experience. My health is suffering, as I have been working late every night and I just don't think I can do this anymore. I applied to a recruitment agency but they never responded. Do you think you can find me another job?'

Philip continued by saying that his current job was his third job in five years and then said, 'I have just had such bad luck with the companies I choose. I have been chatting to a friend of mine, who has been very successful in business, and he suggested that I try to get a job at this *amazing* new start-up company that has done so well in the UK.'

We're not a recruitment agency, but we do help people to help themselves find new jobs. However, in Philip's case we were not yet certain that this was his problem. We decided to take Philip's case because we suspected that the real cause of his career dilemma was one we had often solved.

Nicole

Nicole, a 35-year-old lady whose life had not worked out as she had planned, said it was 'such a shock' when her husband asked for a divorce and left her with the kids. She explained, 'It has been a hard road to travel but I managed to support myself and get through the worst times. My job and the security it provides us have become very important to me, but I feel there is something missing. I feel like I failed at my marriage and I really don't want to fail at my career too. I am sure I can do more in my work. I want to find a job that I enjoy and that also has good financial prospects. Do you think this is possible?'

Of course it's possible, but not without Nicole being able to see what was getting in her way. Nicole was feeling as much trapped by having to support her young family as she was feeling unfulfilled. It's a sad situation that many people find themselves in and, knowing we could help, we took the case immediately.

Kagiso

Kagiso was participating in the graduate programme of a large bank. His father was a miner and his mother a domestic worker. He wanted to maximise himself in the workplace and take advantage of all the opportunities his parents didn't have. He felt as if he was not making progress quickly enough and needed some assistance to get to the top quickly. He asked, 'What can I do to get a promotion? I want to become a manager quickly.'

A lot of people are in a hurry with their careers, particularly younger people who think that, if success does not come quickly, it might not come at all. We're fortunate to have seen success come to people at any age but that's not really what Kagiso was asking us for, although it seemed that way. We suspected that Kagiso's underlying concerns were a little more complicated so we were excited to help him solve his career dilemma.

John

John told us about the two job opportunities he had been offered in his current company and said, 'I don't know which opportunity I should choose. Maybe it's time to start my own thing.' He was not interested in looking into the future and planning. He wanted a good plan for the short term. Option 1 involved managing a team of people on an energy-saving project. Option 2 was a more technical role, getting involved in designing products for energy saving. Option 3 was to start his own business, consulting on energy-saving devices.

We politely explained to John that he appeared to be facing a decision between some short-term options and that we specialise in career dilemmas. We explained that the difference between simply deciding between a few options and actually solving career dilemmas involves taking a long-term view, examining real drivers of happiness, as well as other factors that we explore later in this book. John left, seemingly angry at our viewpoint.

It's not that we didn't want to help; we simply don't think that all career problems or issues are career dilemmas requiring professional assistance.

Two months later, John returned. He said that the more he thought about it, the more he realised that maybe he was trying to solve the wrong problem.

John's experience, or rather our experience with John, reminded us just how easily we can all fall into the trap of confusing real career dilemmas with what feels like 'just a single decision that I'm facing today'. For many people, their career dilemmas *are* a series of short-term decisions that get them into the positions that are making them unhappy.

Tanya

Tanya lived in the USA and wrote an email to us, summarising her career dilemma. She said, 'I'm 24 years old. I applied to nursing school on a whim a few years ago and since then have been, as my friend calls it, "married" to this career. I achieved my qualification and have been working as a cardiology RN in a prestigious Pennsylvania hospital for the past two years. The hospital offers US$8 000 per calendar year for tuition so I have been taking graduate classes to become a family nurse practitioner. At the rate I'm going, I should complete my FNP degree in three years' time.

'At 24, I have a nice car, a house and a loving boyfriend. The only problem is that I think I made the wrong career choice!

'Now I feel like the past six years of my life have been invested in a field I am not sure I want to pursue. On average, I feel like quitting my job every three to four weeks. Once in a while, I come home crying from the stress and workload. It is extremely stressful, not only caring for acutely sick people, but working among the hospital staff as well. As a young nurse, I am treated as incompetent, although I have been told by my clinical specialist that I am one of the best nurses on the floor – so much so that she wants me to transfer to the critical care unit. After two years, I still do not feel as if I fit in.

'In high school, I had the option to take an advanced art class as a major. I loved every minute of it and the work never seemed like *work* to me. I chose not to go for a career in art because it is financially uncertain and I have been financially independent since I was 15.

'Considering the economy, I am afraid to leave nursing but I am simultaneously afraid I will not be brave enough to find a career that truly makes me happy. I feel lost and am not sure if I just haven't found the *right* area of nursing. I feel unsure of myself, isolated in my work and unhappy with nursing overall.'

This is a classic career dilemma, and frankly, all the more difficult to solve as a result. It's so common that, as a society, we've almost come to expect feeling this way. We all make career choices; they don't always match what we love doing, but we have to make a living so we tell ourselves to 'suck it up'. Many people spend their whole careers telling themselves this and it's rare that we come across someone like Tanya who is prepared to make herself vulnerable by being so honest about her position. We knew we could help. Sometimes we get the feeling that we're about to see a life change; that a person is going to blossom. It's these kinds of cases that make us do what we do each day and we had a feeling that Tanya was going to be one of these. Of course, we accepted her case and couldn't wait to get going.

Lutendo

Finally, meet Lutendo.

'I was promised that getting a degree and qualifying as a professional would guarantee me a job. I have a huge student loan and my parents want me to move out. I am feeling a bit desperate. I am starting to get scared that I might just have to accept whatever offer I get. Or that I might not get an offer at all.'

Like a growing number of people, Lutendo's career dilemma was that he had no career and he couldn't find one. Or at least he couldn't find a *job* (often confused with a *career*). We usually help people who are stuck in one career and want to change or fix something. Sometimes people are between jobs, but Lutendo was just starting out and a first misstep can often be the biggest cause of unhappiness (as we saw with Tanya). Working with Lutendo was an opportunity for us to help him take his first career steps powerfully and avoid the many pitfalls and ruts that so many of our clients find themselves in before reaching out for help.

WHAT WE WANT YOU TO NOTICE

Notice that the details of these career dilemmas may be unique but the basic themes represent the many career dilemmas being experienced in our world. Notice people struggling to find enjoyment and meaning in their work; people struggling to keep out of The Trap of working only to pay the bills. Notice the pain, frustration, fear, indecision and uncertainty experienced by many in this situation. Notice that people often don't know who to turn to or how to move forward.

In an effort to assist career navigators to move from unconscious incompetence to conscious competence, we have highlighted certain thought and behaviour patterns that prevent people from navigating their careers more effectively. You may recognise some or all of them in yourself too.

AVOIDANCE OF RESPONSIBILITY

Many people have a tendency to blame others for their career troubles and avoid taking responsibility themselves. They blame their teachers, parents, recruiters, HR managers and bosses. They ignore the active role that successful people play in creating successful careers.

We can see this behaviour in Philip's story. He avoided taking responsibility for his career and looked outward to blame bad luck and other people for his career troubles. The easiest way forward for him was to blame his employer and to jump ship *again*.

Do you realise that it is your responsibility to manage your career? Maybe you mistakenly thought your employer would manage it, helping you to develop as they have succession plans and will need managers in the future. We met with thought leaders and human resource directors to understand the company's position in the current world of work. They all agreed that the responsibility for managing and developing a career now sits with the *individual*. They also agreed that it is the company's responsibility to support the individual in this process and to provide the necessary opportunities, but that's where it ends. Essentially, they're all saying, 'You're on your own, buddy.'

Nick Binedell, founding director of the Gordon Institute of Business Science, supports this position by saying, 'It is possible for human resources, mentors and advisors to provide a "menu" of development options and to support an individual in their choice. However it is only the individual who can "order and eat the food."'

Clearly a company needs to develop a leadership pipeline for its future management and leadership. To achieve this and all succession planning objectives, it should be prepared to provide employees with opportunities for development. However, its objectives for a person may differ from his career goals and desires. For a successful future together, the individual will need to decide if there is sufficient overlap between his personal career goals and the company's plans for his development.

Companies expect people to step up and take the opportunities offered. Companies are there for shareholders and customers first, and they're looking for employees who think like they do and put the company, its clients and shareholders first. That's fine as a shared value, but the dark side of this expectation is that many people feel that looking after their own needs first is somehow selfish or against corporate values. We could not disagree more. We think that the *first* and most important way to serve customers, shareholders and your employer is to make sure that you're in the right career, in the right job, in the right environment and showing up to work each day, powerfully in action and unstoppably committed to doing your best. If that's not you, you're not serving anyone!

And then there is always the question, 'What if the company's next plan doesn't include me?' For many, the realisation may be forced upon them and it is frightening not knowing what to do. This is what happened to one of our clients on a quiet Tuesday afternoon: Janet arrived at our door with desperation in her eyes after a major bank retrenched over 3 000 employees. Clearly still in shock she said, 'I worked there for 20 years and it's all that I have ever known. They just deactivated my access card.' She continued, 'I thought I would always work there. I don't know what to do next.'

Lifetime employment is over. Technology now allows for many more workplace arrangements and development options. As a result, companies have passed the responsibility of managing and navigating careers to the employees. You may ask why. In short, they have done it in the hope of increasing employees' engagement in the workplace. They are hoping that, if employees are required to make the choices, they will become more interested and engaged in their work. Moreover, as more and more people are seeking jobs, companies are better served replacing demotivated people with people who really want to be there and who love what they're doing. It no longer makes sense to try to make employees happy. Rather, find employees who will be happy doing what needs to be done, then leave them to manage their own careers.

Currently this new mindset is giving rise to an unprecedented number of career dilemmas but in the longer term, once we all become consciously competent in career navigation, it may well increase engagement.

LOOKING OUTWARD FOR SOLUTIONS

Many people tend to hope that someone or something will help them to find career success, even if they don't understand what they have to offer or know what they want in a job. They *think* that they know themselves, understand what they like and can judge what they're good at. They *think* they know what they're looking for in a job and that they can articulate it if asked. It's just something they feel they know about themselves.

Finish these five sentences, but do it in writing on a separate piece of paper:
- What I like about my current job is ...
- What I'm good at is ...
- What I look for in an ideal job is ...
- My best contribution would be in a job which ...
- How I add value in my ideal job is by ...

Could you do this task in a few minutes, or did it take some thinking? What would happen if someone asked you questions like this at a chance meeting, at a dinner party or in an elevator? Would you answer that person confidently and quickly?

Now take your answers, give them to someone else and ask that person to read them back to you. Are you hearing someone you would want to employ right now, on the spot, at any price? If not, you might have your own career dilemma. In fact, if you're reading this book, there is a good chance you've already come to that conclusion.

Tanya did not know what she had to offer the world and said that she had become very unsure of herself. She is part of the so-called Generation Y, known to be much less accepting of work that doesn't fulfil them and their needs. To avoid career dilemmas and endless job-hopping, she too would need to look inward before looking outward, and be very clear about what she had to offer the world of work.

We saw that Philip didn't know what he had to offer a future employer or what he wanted in a job. He wanted someone else to find him suitable work. He looked to a recruitment company (outward) before considering what he wanted to do or what he had to offer (inward). He had no idea of his career goals or what work would excite or motivate him to be his best.

Philip, like most jobseekers, turned to a recruitment agency. Some recruitment agencies are very capable and do make an effort to provide appropriate guidance to jobseekers. However the majority want to place you in a job as quickly as possible to earn their commission, and would be happy to do it again next year.

It is unrealistic to expect the average recruitment agency to sort out your career dilemma without you being able to answer some basic questions including, 'What are you looking for?', 'What do you have to offer a company?' and 'What are you good at doing?' Even then, let's be clear, if you're paying someone to find you a job, you go to a recruitment agency. If you want to build a satisfying *career*, you're going to have to do a lot of the work yourself.

Reading this book won't, on its own, solve your career dilemma but it can show you how to do the work that will. Prepare yourself because it's going to take some time and a lot of effort – the two things that most people with career dilemmas consistently avoid investing.

LACK OF TIME AND EFFORT SPENT

Many people know that their career choices affect so many aspects of their lives yet they spend very little time actively managing these.

Isn't it strange that people's jobs allow them to buy cars, but that they often give the choice of car more attention than the choice of jobs they have? The average person spends about 65 minutes a year actively planning his career. That's about one quarter of the time we spend thinking about a new car or looking at alternatives when it comes time to buy one.

Any surprise, therefore, that most people feel like they're not in control of their careers?

John simply wanted to decide upon one of the options and move forward. He didn't seem to want to spend the time or effort really understanding himself, what each option involved and what would allow him to be engaged.

LACK OF CAREER-MANAGEMENT SKILLS AND KNOWLEDGE

Career navigation is complex, as each individual brings a unique set of skills, values, interests and experiences to the process of designing and managing his career. Most people lack the set of non-occupational skills, knowledge and attitudes for career navigation. It's for this reason that we decided to write this book – to share these skills and processes that are simply not a part of formal education and certainly not a part of on-the-job training.

Career navigators, like you, need skills to understand themselves and the value they contribute to a company. They need skills to identify and create opportunities that are suitable for them in the world of work. They need skills to identify job opportunities as well as the most effective learning and development opportunities.

You may think career navigation skills are obvious. If you look around and see the number of career dilemmas in our society, it's clear that this is not so.

This is evident in all the career dilemma stories that we have started to share. Both Philip and Tanya required skill and knowledge to understand themselves and what work would fulfil them; Nicole required skill and knowledge to generate and evaluate career alternatives, and John required skill and knowledge to evaluate his options and choose powerfully. Lutendo, like so many other career navigators, lacked the skills and knowledge to create the right opportunity for himself.

LACK OF KNOWLEDGEABLE GUIDANCE

Many people look to successful friends or wise family to assist them in overcoming their career dilemmas. The world of work has become too complex to rely only on the guidance of well-meaning friends and family.

Philip turned to his 'successful' friend for guidance. Maybe he would have been given worthwhile guidance but maybe not. Many people look to family members. Some, like Kagiso, know that their family don't have the necessary context and understanding to help them. Others discover that the experience their families do have is now outdated or irrelevant in the new, fast-paced globalised world. Loving, caring friends and family are also often blinded by how they feel towards you, and as a result can't be as honest (or brutal, when that's what's required) as you need them to be.

Whatever the reason, people like Kagiso require independent assistance to create a game plan for becoming their best. A new strategy with more knowledgeable players is needed.

WHAT THIS MEANS FOR YOU

There is good news in all of this for you (as there was for the six people we've introduced). Your current ineffectiveness in navigating your career is likely resulting more from a lack of skills and knowledge of the navigation process than your incompetence in your work or personal deficiencies. It's hard to admit that you might not have these skills, but if you're unhappy in your career and it's been this way for a while, lower your defences for a bit and read on to discover what skills you may be missing.

The solution to overcoming career dilemmas lies in obtaining skills and knowledge and some new mindsets to navigate your career. Anyone can become a powerful career navigator because the tools are relatively simple to master. You don't have to wait for everyone and everything else to change – you can be the change yourself.

So join us as we share with you how we helped our clients answer their common question, 'How can I better navigate my career?' We will show you how our principles, tools and techniques helped them to solve their career dilemmas, and we will teach you how to apply the same method to your own dilemma.

COACHES' CORNER

Write a paragraph describing your career dilemma. Answer the following as honestly as you can:

- Review your dilemma and identify any of the five thought or behaviour patterns discussed in this chapter that may be holding you back.
- What impact are these thoughts and behaviours having on you and your career?
- What are you going to do to change these thoughts or behaviour?

MAIN POINTS

Five thought and behaviour patterns, evident in most career dilemmas may be preventing you from effectively navigating your career. These are:

- Avoidance of responsibility;
- Looking outward for solutions;
- Lack of time and effort spent;
- Lack of career-management skills and knowledge;
- Lack of knowledgeable guidance.

The solution to overcoming your career dilemma lies in obtaining skills and knowledge, and adopting new mindsets to navigate your career more effectively.

2

THE CAREER NAVIGATION MODEL

'Twenty years from now you will be more disappointed
by the things that you didn't do than by the ones you did do.
So throw off the bowlines. Sail away from the safe harbour.
Catch the trade winds in your sails. Explore. Dream. Discover.'

Mark Twain

Explorers through the ages travelled into wild unknown territory, seeking new lands, wealth and adventure. No maps existed. They were forced to forge their own paths. They had to endure tough conditions and develop crucial survival skills without a guarantee that they would find what they were looking for or come back alive. What kept them going was their dedication to their mission, their preparation and their resourcefulness. These kept them looking for clues and encouraged them to cooperate (and sometimes compete) with other explorers – always sharpening their skills, navigating obstacles and believing they would find what they were looking for.

As a career navigator in these very turbulent times, you are sometimes going to feel like those explorers. And, like them, you're going to have to have a well-equipped survival toolkit.

THE EXPLORER'S TOOLKIT:
The Career Navigation Model

Explorers sometimes don't have maps; the terrain that they have to travel over might be unfamiliar to them. But every successful explorer or navigator has had at least two key things: a sense of purpose (knowing the destination or the outcome of their quest) and a strong toolkit (including resources, skills, companions and resourcefulness) that they have used to navigate both the known and unknown sections of the journey.

You might be very clear in your mind about what your ideal career looks like, or you might be starting with a vague idea. You might feel you have all the skills, knowledge and drive you need to reach your goal, or you might not even have an idea of what you'll need to succeed. Wherever you find yourself, this book is designed to help you build your toolkit as you navigate your career journey.

Kerry and her team have spent many years developing the Career Navigation Model to help people navigate their careers successfully in the changing world of work. It aims to create career navigators who are engaged, committed to being their best and actively moving towards achieving their career desires.

The stages of the model are set out briefly below, and explained in detail in later chapters.

Stage 1: Understand yourself

In the same way that a business takes stock of its assets, you need to understand your assets, primarily your capabilities and desires. You want to know where you are at your best, what you have to offer a company or team, what your work preferences are, what engages your heart and mind, and what you are hoping to achieve through your career. You want to look inward before looking outward.

Stage 2: Understand the world of work

The world of work is changing rapidly and you need to be informed about current trends and opportunities, as well as those that are likely to exist in the coming years. You want to know what other navigators and players are doing and the plans they are making to maximise their opportunities in the future world of work. Being aware of emerging trends and opportunities does not mean constantly looking for a career change. Rather, it means looking for ways to make whatever career you choose maximally successful.

Stage 3: Create possibilities

With a greater understanding of self and the world of work, you can find, create and develop suitable options in the world of work. This stage allows you to explore exactly what you want to do, what roles you want to play and what impact you want to have on the world. It is a time of trial and exploration. It is a time to test your understanding of self and the world of work, and to develop a network. It is a time to understand how your capabilities compare to others and identify your own uniqueness. It is a time to reflect and learn. It is a time to clarify and a time to make connections.

Stage 4: Make it happen

This stage requires you to take action to make your desires a reality. You will use all the resources at your disposal to make it happen for you. This does not mean that you can make anything happen, or that you need to do it all yourself. But it does require you to take responsibility for your actions and attitudes, and to have the initiative to make your career choices and desires a reality.

Stage 5: Become your best

You want to become your best and achieve lifetime employability by honing your skills, building your capabilities and securing career-enhancing opportunities. Successful career navigators seek to continually build on their advantage. The goal is not just your next job or promotion. Rather, you want to reach a point of being confidently calm about your future career, knowing that, by being a successful career navigator, you will always be able to find work that is fulfilling, rewarding and allows you to make a contribution.

THE EXPLORER'S TOOLKIT:
Four Mindsets of Successful Career Navigators

As you take responsibility for your career and bravely accept that it is a journey into the wild unknown, you need to be prepared to do what it takes to find your desired treasure. To ensure that you reach your destination and avoid The Trap, we recommend that you adopt four important mindsets.

A mindset is a belief or a way of looking at the world. Your mindsets and beliefs have a huge impact on your behaviour and, as a result, your success. Adopting a new mindset is as easy as simply deciding to do it. What is difficult is *remembering* your new mindset when you're faced with daily challenges. That's when people often revert back to their old (and often false) views about how the world works. That's when they say things like 'It was his fault that …' and forget that they had agreed with themselves to adopt a new mindset. When navigating your career, we suggest that four key mindset shifts are necessary starting points.

Mindset 1: My career is my responsibility

It is your responsibility to understand yourself and the world of work; generate possible career and job options; evaluate those options and choose the one that will allow you to have your desired impact on the world. It is also your responsibility to actively seek skills, knowledge and career-enhancing opportunities that will allow you to become your best.

Taking responsibility does not mean you have to do this alone. There are many others who might share your journey and even help you along the way. Taking responsibility also does not mean that things will happen only because you make them happen. Sometimes lucky things do just happen; sometimes events take a course that you cannot anticipate or control. But in every situation, your mindset needs to be one of personal responsibility. This is *your* career and *you* need to make it happen. This is a vital starting point for navigating your career successfully. Without this, nothing else in these pages will work, and you're likely to give up when things get tough, blaming others for your sense of failure.

Consider the six people we introduced you to in Chapter 1. Philip and Lutendo might both have been battling with this mindset, as they looked to blame external circumstances for their situations. Philip found it easier to blame his employers than to look at his own shortcomings as a potential manager. Lutendo found it easier to blame a weak economy and society than to discover how he might have enhanced his education to make himself more employable. You'll discover through the book how Philip and Lutendo began to take responsibility, and learn some of the steps that helped them as they worked through the five stages of our Career Navigation Model. But for now, just know that one of the most important early steps for both of them was to accept responsibility for their own careers.

Before you carry on reading, take a moment to ask yourself if you *really* believe that you have this mindset. Do you genuinely believe that your career is your responsibility? Can you list three specific actions you've taken in the last few months that prove you have this mindset? Or are you waiting, hoping that someone else will intervene? If so, who is it and why would they? And do you really believe that's going to happen?

Ideas for adopting this mindset

There are many books entirely devoted to helping people change their mindsets. At the risk, then, of being a bit simplistic, here are a few suggestions for you if you feel that you need to do a better job of accepting responsibility for your own career:

- Once you've done a little bit of work on our five-stage plan (at least the first three stages), make a specific note on a blank piece of paper. The note should simply be a description of the type of work you would like to be doing five years from now. Stick the note up in a place where you'll see it regularly (like your fridge or the bathroom mirror). There's no magic to doing this, but trust us: it works. It is a daily reminder of what you've decided to do. Sceptical? Go on, try it anyway. What's the worst that could happen?
- Tell a trusted friend or family member your career ambition for the next five years. Ask that person to ask you about what you've done towards it at least once every six months.
- Read *The Brand You 50: Reinventing Work* by Tom Peters (Alfred A Knopf, 1999).

- Subscribe to Brazen Careerist (www.brazencareerist.com) and read their articles on taking responsibility for your career.
- Identify a role model who does take responsibility for his career. Watch and learn from that person's actions and behaviours.

Mindset 2: I learn

Based on decades of research into achievement and success, Carol Dweck, a world-renowned Stanford University psychologist, teaches in her book, *Mindset: How You Can Fulfil Your Potential* (Robinson, 2012), that a growth mindset makes all the difference in achieving success.

She defines a mindset as 'a belief about how the world works, and [your] role in it'. She describes a fixed mindset as a 'belief that your qualities are carved in stone creating an urgency to prove yourself over and over' and a growth mindset as the 'belief that your basic qualities are things you can cultivate through your efforts'. Carol Dweck is very clear in her beliefs about what this growth mindset can help people to achieve: 'Although people may differ in every which way – in their initial thoughts and aptitudes, interests or temperaments – everyone can change and grow through application and experience.'

Your mindsets affect your behaviours and actions. Carol Dweck's research shows that those with a growth mindset are more likely to stretch themselves, take on challenges and move out of their comfort zones in an effort to improve and grow, and as a result, are more likely to succeed than those with a fixed mindset. Interestingly, it is often very talented individuals who develop a fixed mindset and avoid moving out of their comfort zones in case they expose their deficiencies.

The good news is that you can change your mindset and develop a new set of thoughts and behaviours. As a successful career navigator, you should adopt an 'I learn' mindset and develop a passion for learning. By doing this, you give yourself permission to fail and make mistakes without judging yourself a failure. You give yourself permission to explore, experiment and grow. You focus on the learning process. You release yourself from the need to be perfect and you silence your ego.

The most dominant and often the most successful player in career dilemmas is fear. Through its domination, it dictates the way forward, limits your actions and prevents you from stretching yourself. Fear is more prevalent in a fixed mindset and as you take on the mindset of 'I learn', you will accept that failure is an important part of growth and stretching yourself out of your comfort zone. Those who have done great things, such as Thomas Edison, are often those who have also failed on many occasions.

Tanya would have benefited from adopting this mindset. She would have avoided labelling herself a failure (which is common with a fixed mindset) and rather identified what she had learnt from her experiences, allowing herself to move forward. Those with a fixed mindset are prone to inaction and feeling sorry for themselves, which may involve drinking heavily, staying in bed, watching TV excessively and avoiding taking any steps forward.

Ideas for adopting this mindset

- In his excellent book for entrepreneurs, *The E-Myth Revisited* (HarperCollins, 1994), Michael E Gerber coined the phrase, 'work ON your business, not IN your business'. By this, he meant that too many small business owners spend too much of their time just doing work to run their businesses (fulfilling orders, chasing clients, doing admin, etc) and don't spend enough time thinking about how to grow their businesses by stepping back. The same is true of most people in their careers. They spend all their time just doing their jobs, just a bit of time trying to get a promotion, but almost no time at all on developing their careers. By reading this book, you're actually taking a few good steps to correct this mistake, but what else can you do to develop your understanding of your career? If you could meet anyone, who would you choose to meet to learn more about the future you desire? Can you do anything to meet this person?
- One of the most powerful tools for learning in the 21st century is the concept of *un*learning. It's quite easy to identify new skills, information or attitudes that you might need to learn, but it's another altogether to try to identify those things within yourself that are no longer useful or helpful. These might be habits, actions, attitudes or even relationships that you must firmly place in the bin of your history, let go and unlearn.

What do you need to unlearn? Go on, take a few minutes and make a list.

- Read the book *Mindset: How You Can Fulfil Your Potential* (Robinson, 2012) and take the test to identify your current mindset. You could also listen to Carol Dweck's ideacast (http://blogs.hbr.org/ideacast/2012/01/the-right-mindset-for-success.html) to understand more about the implications of a mindset.
- In everything you do (including your latest project, team meeting, client presentation and current job), identify what you are learning and decide what you want to do with that learning.
- Notice when you limit your growth by choosing to stay in your comfort zone. Consciously choose growth as opposed to comfort.

Mindset 3: I create career success

By adopting this mindset, you accept that your actions, attitudes and hard work will determine how you experience and engage with the world around you. The perfect career opportunity is not somewhere 'out there'; it is within your grasp. Career navigators need to use their unique resources and experiences to create new and better alternatives.

The psychological term 'internal locus of control' refers to the belief that you can control events that affect you, or that even if external circumstances are beyond your control, you can control how you respond to them. Your career outcomes result more from your own behaviour than external forces. People with an internal locus of control believe that they can influence their career outcomes through hard work, good attitudes and smart decisions. Adopting this mindset requires you to recognise that the position (the locus) of your control is within you. If you believe that your career outcomes result mainly from external forces (you have an external locus of control), you may want to spend some time developing more of an internal locus of control.

Humans have the unique ability to imagine things and this gives people the power to change their worlds. You can imagine what you most want to *be*, what need you want to meet, what talent you want to use, and then take small steps towards achieving your vision.

Kagiso is an example of someone who demonstrated a good grasp of this mindset. He was confident that he could be successful in his career, and was seeking out assistance to make that a reality. Creating career success does not mean that you do it all by yourself – sometimes you do need help – but the mindset is that it is up to you to take the initiative. Nicole, for instance, would benefit greatly from taking on this mindset.

Kerry was driving with her seven-year-old daughter to school early one morning. As her daughter had just started to read, she read all the signboards on the journey out loud. The one board read, 'Be anything you want to be.' Kerry was so excited as this was going to be the moment when she got to share her belief with her precious daughter – that you can choose who you want to be in your life and your career. Kerry wasn't going to allow her to constrain herself by considering limited possibilities. Before Kerry could say another word, her daughter said very indignantly, 'That is not true, is it, Mom? Because I want to be a fairy and I can't.'

She was right, of course. Graeme, for example, would have loved to be a professional cricketer, but with his bad hand-eye coordination, that was never going to be an option. Peter Ndoro, a TV presenter and journalist has said that, growing up in the UK, he would have loved to be an English bobby (foot patrol policeman) but you have to be 5'10" tall to be accepted. He even ate more to encourage this upward growth, but never achieved the qualifying height.

Creating your own reality is not about living in a fantasy world. You'll see as you read on that you need a very sober and frank view of your own skills and abilities. But there are always more options than appear evident at first glance, when people get to choose how their dreams and desires manifest themselves.

So, yes, there are some constraints on everyone's lives and career options, but there is still so much more possibility that many people don't allow themselves to consider. There is no 'best career choice' for an individual. Rather, an individual has the resources to pursue many alternative career paths.

Making use of this mindset can allow career navigators to break out of their current realities and create many new possibilities for themselves.

Ideas for adopting this mindset

- You may want to start by assessing your current locus of control. You can find a test for assessing your locus of control and some strategies for changing it on www.mindtools.com.
- Read *The Law of Success in Sixteen Lessons* by Napoleon Hill (BN Publishing, 2007).

- Identify a role model who has this mindset. Watch and learn from that person's behaviours. If possible, speak to your role model about his views on creating success.
- Read *The Art of Possibility* by Rosamund Stone Zander and Benjamin Zander (Penguin Books, 2002).
- Watch Dr John Demartini's YouTube video *Master Planning for Life* (www. youtube.com/watch?v=WMa3z0p6YX4).
- Watch the YouTube video of J K Rowling's Commencement Speech at Harvard in 2008 (www.youtube.com/watch?v=nkREt4ZB-ck).

Mindset 4: I seek to be engaged

Engaged career navigators bring their hearts, hands and heads to their work. They bring *all their discretionary energy* to tasks and involve the wholeness of themselves. This drastically increases their chances of success in the workplace.

A bored and frustrated worker who stares into space not knowing or caring about the quality or outcomes of his work has a very low level of engagement and brings as little as possible of himself to the workplace. This worker is unlikely to be considered for pay increases, promotions, or other career-enhancing opportunities.

Heroes, as they leave to go to battle, or missionaries, as they save people's lives, have a very high level of engagement and involve their hearts, heads and hands in achieving their goals. In a similar way, highly engaged career navigators bring all their discretionary energy to securing a deal, managing a client issue, operating on a patient or developing a new idea. These career navigators are much more likely to be considered for bonuses, promotions and career-enhancing opportunities.

Think for a moment of particular people you know who are completely engaged in their work. They have energy when others are tired. They are persistent when others give up and work tirelessly towards their goal. This behaviour, of being engaged, is more likely to lead to success and recognition than half-heartedness and lack of interest. Successful career navigators seek to bring the best of themselves to their work and, in so doing, give themselves the greatest chance of success.

While watching successful career navigators, we have become aware that being engaged is partly chosen (as an attitude) and is partly a function of how closely aligned these people's talents, skills, interests, values and goals are to their current work opportunities. Understanding and accepting your talents, skills, interests, values and goals increases the chances of securing an opportunity that will allow you to be engaged.

So often, career navigators blame employers or their situation for their low levels of engagement in their work. Successful career navigators know that being engaged in their work is their responsibility, and seek or create opportunities that allow for engagement.

Kagiso showed us how the use of this mindset determined his next steps. When Kagiso started as a graduate in a large South African bank, he watched his boss, Steven, working to solve system problems. Steven was so focused that he was in the office early and worked consistently for most of the day. Kagiso noticed that Steven was interested in the detail – making sure his work was correct – and he became excited when he managed to restore the system. Kagiso watched and learnt everything he could. Steven was promoted and Kagiso was given his role.

Kagiso wanted to follow in his boss's footsteps. In the first week, he felt good as he was just like Steven and he felt excited about his future prospects. As the weeks passed, he noticed he was a little late for work each day and was less focused. It was not noticeable to his new boss but he knew it. As he was serious about his career and wanted to be excellent in this role, like Steven was, he decided to meet with Steven and ask him his secret. Steven said, 'Secret? I don't have a secret. I just love solving each issue until the system works. Don't you?' Kagiso knew that he didn't. He had not found the same level of intrinsic value in his work that Steven had and as a result was not as engaged.

Kagiso learnt that, even though he wanted to be engaged, it takes effort, trial, and sometimes error to find the role or work that transforms someone from a bored and frustrated worker into an involved and engaged person.

Daniel H Pink's book, *Drive: The Surprising Truth About What Motivates Us* (Canongate Books, 2010) highlights the fact that the best motivators are intrinsic. This means that people are motivated more by things that are inside them (things they care about, and things that interest and excite them) than by external factors (such as money, rewards or threats). At work, they know that intrinsic motivators are more effective motivators than a system of command and control. Being engaged requires you to understand your own intrinsic motivators and navigate your career with these in mind.

Both John and Philip would have benefited from adopting this mindset. It would ensure that they chose work in the future that would allow them to be engaged and bring the best of themselves to their work. Many career navigators are so focused on maximising salary and bonuses that they forget that they will need to do the work and would benefit in the short and longer term by choosing the job option that allows them to be engaged.

Ideas for adopting this mindset

- Observe those who are engaged in their work and notice the impact on their lives, their energy, their health and their career success. Their energy and passion should encourage you to adopt this mindset.
- Notice when you blame others for your boring job. *Stop* the blaming and ask yourself what you need to change to become more engaged.
- Decide to be more engaged on a particular day and see what happens. Notice what reduces your level of engagement and what raises it.
- Remember a time when you were engaged. What were you doing? How did it affect your energy levels and fulfilment?
- Read *Go Put Your Strengths to Work* by Marcus Buckingham (Simon & Schuster, 2007). Alternatively, visit www.simplystrengths.com for a strengths engagement tracker, which can assist you in monitoring your engagement and the use of your strengths.
- Visit the website www.ted.com to witness people from many different fields being engaged in their work and speaking passionately about their interests. Their energy and enthusiasm is contagious!

WHAT THIS MEANS FOR YOU

The route is now laid out in front of you. Your new mindsets ensure that you are in the driver's seat, believing you can achieve career success and always seeking to learn. What remains is to manage your expectations about this journey. If you look at the path of any successful career navigator, you will see effort and perseverance. Sadly, there doesn't seem to be a shortcut to success. The journey you are about to embark on will demand everything you have available to you. But that is okay as this journey is your chance to make a contribution and to be more than you ever dreamt possible. This is your chance to escape The Trap that holds so many people back.

COACHES' CORNER

Complete the coaching exercises below to practise adopting the mindsets.

Mindset 1: My career is my responsibility

Review the following list and note who you may have blamed for your career difficulties in the past: Parents, lecturers or teachers, mentors, friends, recruiters, human resources, past employers or bosses, politicians, peers, or other races or genders.

- Have you blamed anyone else?
- What has been the impact of this on your career?
- What actions would you take if you really believed that your career was your responsibility?
- What would you stop doing if you really believed that your career was your responsibility?

Mindset 2: I learn

Remember a time when you made a mistake and it made you feel like a failure.

- Looking back, what did you learn from the mistake?
- How does that learning benefit you?
- How does this learning increase your value to a company?
- What will you do differently in the future as a result of this learning?
- If you had an adopted the mindset of 'I learn', how would your reaction have been different? What impact would that have had on you and those around you?

Mindset 3: I create career success

Imagine a perfect day at work.

- What need would you be meeting?
- What task would you be doing?
- What work conditions would you like?
- What work experiences will you have had?
- What would success in this day look like?
- What would people say about you?
- Do you believe that you could create this perfect day? If you answered no to this question, maybe your mindset, and not external forces, is holding you back from achieving career success. Work on developing a more internal locus of control.

Mindset 4: I seek to be engaged

- Identify the activities or times when you are engaged at work.
- What are you doing? What are you enjoying about those activities?
- Notice how you are more engaged when you are working in your areas of strengths or talents.
- How can you change your role to allow you to be more engaged (if not immediately, then over time)?

MAIN POINTS

As a career navigator you need to don your explorer's hat and get ready to do what it takes to navigate your career.

The Career Navigation Model requires you to obtain a better understanding of yourself and the world of work. Using this understanding, you actively seek to create possibilities for which you are uniquely suited. You then need to take action to make one or more of these possibilities a reality. You will need to hone your skills and continually build on your advantage to remain relevant in the rapidly changing world of work.

Four new mindsets were recommended for successful career navigation, namely:

My career is my responsibility

It is my responsibility to understand myself and the world of work, generate possible career and job options, evaluate those options and powerfully choose the option that will allow me to have my desired impact on the world.

I learn

I give myself permission to learn, explore and experiment even if it means making some mistakes.

I create career success

I accept that I play a major role in creating my reality and I empower myself to create my own reality. I accept that my choices, actions, attitudes and hard work will determine my reality.

I seek to be engaged

I seek to bring all my discretionary energy to my tasks as this will increase my chances of success and recognition. I also seek tasks that will allow me to do this more easily.

SUGGESTED READING

Mindset by Carol Dweck (Ballantine Books, 2006)

Drive: The Surprising Truth about What Motivates Us by Daniel Pink (Canongate Books, 2010)

The Brand You 50: Reinventing Work by Tom Peters (Alfred A Knopf, 1999)

The Art of Possibility by Rosamund Stone Zander and Benjamin Zander (Penguin Books, 2002)

The Law of Success in Sixteen Lessons by Napoleon Hill (BN Publishing, 2007)

3

STAGE 1: UNDERSTANDING YOU

'I don't like that man. I must get to know him better.'
Abraham Lincoln

'Whatever the circumstances of your life, the understanding
of type can make your perceptions clearer, your judgements
sounder and your life closer to your heart's desire.'
Isabel Briggs Myers

You've lived with yourself your whole life, and every time you look in the mirror, there you are. And yet, this is no guarantee that you know yourself. In fact, it's fairly clear that the vast majority of people don't know themselves as well as they should, and this is one of the key reasons they have not found fulfilling careers. Stage 1 of your navigation to a new career is to understand yourself.

Like most of those around you, you may know some things about yourself from your performance appraisals or from the ranting and raving (or praises and commendations) of your parents, partner or boss. You've probably also completed two or three of those quick tests in a glossy magazine, and feel they have provided some insights into who you are. You may have done some psychometric tests in the past but the results are probably buried in a drawer somewhere.

However you've acquired it, you probably have some knowledge about your personality and unique attributes. Maybe, for example, you are more extroverted than introverted; maybe you prefer routine to creative work, or maybe you are good with people. There is so much information about who you are that you can easily be overwhelmed or confused by it. The only safe bet, we're sure, is that you are not using all this information about yourself to your maximum advantage.

That is all about to change. The first stage of the Career Navigation Model is to understand yourself, so you need to gather as much information about yourself as possible and even investigate aspects of yourself that you may have never considered before. The key is not to get more and more data about yourself. Rather, you need to get enough of the right *type* of information and ensure you cover all the attributes that make up a fully rounded human being. It might feel like a lot of unnecessary work, as you begin to discover yourself, but it's a vital starting point. It will help you to make better and more informed career development choices (such as choosing a business partner or a team) and show you what you need to be engaged.

Before we tell you *how* to do this, though, it will be useful to know *why* you need to.

WHY YOU NEED IT

If you have a good *working* understanding of self, you know what drives your behaviour and what fulfils you. You know when you can be relied upon and when it is likely that you will crumble (as we all do at times). You are confident about what situations will bring out your best, and you're aware of those that will bring out your worst. You are able to answer the question, 'What do I want in a job?' You have direction and purpose, knowing what career success is for you. You see your blind spots more clearly and understand what has previously held you back from career success.

In the workplace, you know what value you can bring to a project, company or team. You are easily able to choose a role that will suit you and where you can be engaged. You are able to be more consistent and build excellence in your chosen area. You are able to make development decisions that are in line with your needs and direction, thereby making better use of the money spent by your employer on learning and development interventions.

Most importantly, when your work and your entire being are aligned, your work feels fulfilling and enriching. You are the best *you* possible. This clarity of self and your desires empowers you. It gives you self-confidence, purpose and much greater strength for the journey. It provides you with a hard-to-match competitive advantage while many other career navigators fumble in the dark.

If that sounds appealing, you need to understand that there is some hard work to do before you achieve your dream job. Once again, we encourage you not just to read through this book, but to do the exercises we recommend, and to complete as much of the profiling tool we're about to present before moving on to Stage 2.

GETTING THE COMPLETE PICTURE

The goal of this first stage is to bring together all the relevant information you know (or may need to go and find) about yourself to create a *working* understanding of self and identify your career drivers.

A career driver is a behaviour, desire, preference or basic trait that becomes relevant when navigating your career and seeking engagement. All career navigators have differing career drivers and, at different times of their lives, their career drivers may well change. Career drivers may include factors normally tested in psychometric tests, such as personality, interests and values, but they are also likely to include other factors such as work preferences, work hours and network.

To assist you in this process, we suggest using the Self-Q tool (see overleaf). It is a relatively easy-to-complete framework for gathering information from different sources (including previously completed psychometric test results, career assessments, and your own as well as others' opinions). It can be adjusted to include all the relevant information you have at your disposal. Once you have completed the Self-Q tool (see Coaches' Corner for how to do this), you will have gained a working understanding of self and you will be better placed to identify your career drivers.

The Self-Q tool will not perform a complicated calculation and magically determine the perfect career. We're sceptical about 'black box' tools that suggest careers based directly on your answers to a questionnaire, as many of your career decisions depend upon your stage in life and what you define as career success. Instead, we've found that the answers are more complicated and require you to dig a little within yourself. The Self-Q tool guides you in this endeavour.

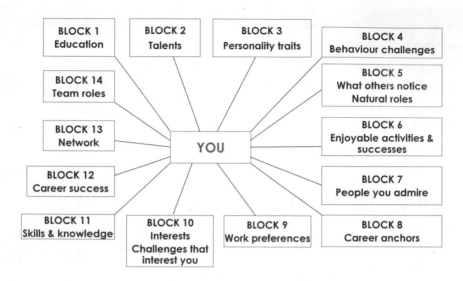

You can make the Self-Q tool as detailed as you prefer. If you are a meticulous person, you may want to include as much detail as possible in each block. We have suggested tests that may help you to do this (see Coaches' Corner). If, however, you prefer the big picture then you may only want to include the pertinent points and move to looking at the whole more quickly – just make sure you have something captured in each block. The main objective is to be able to see a clearer and more complete picture of yourself, and then to be able to identify your career drivers. We suggest that you use the Self-Q tool to support you, rather than drown you.

An example: Philip

Below is the Self-Q tool for Philip, who you met in Chapter 1.

We started Philip's career navigation process by completing the Self-Q tool. Kerry started with Philip's education block and he completed this easily as he had a Bachelor of Commerce, majoring in accounts. He was well educated and we were off to a good start. Next, Kerry introduced the concept of talents. He put his head into his hands and shook his head. He said in a deep gruff voice, 'I am not good at anything. I keep missing my work deadlines.' With a big breath he said, 'My family complains that I don't get things done and the car keeps breaking down. I am not good at anything.'

Without knowing Philip very well, Kerry was still certain he was wrong so, after consoling him, we went back to the Self-Q tool. We decided to skip the talents block and moved to assessments of Philip's personality. He had recently completed a Myers-Briggs Temperament Indicator® and understood he was an ENFP. This meant that he was an *Extrovert* (got his energy from being with people), was *iNtuitive* (liked to see the big picture), made decisions on the basis of *Feelings* (including personal values and what is important to others) and was *Perceiving* (liked to live life in a flexible and spontaneous way, making it up as he went along). This profile helped him to identify some behaviour challenges as well as what others notice about him (mainly positives).

After the initial struggle, Philip started to gain momentum. Slowly, Kerry could feel him becoming more involved in the process and sitting up a little straighter. He even made a joke or two. It took some time, a few assessments and some reading. For his talents block, for example, we used Gallup's excellent StrengthsFinder profile – the cost of this which is the price of the book by the same name. After some reflection and discussion, Philip found an honest contribution for each block.

This is what his Self-Q tool looked like once he had finished:

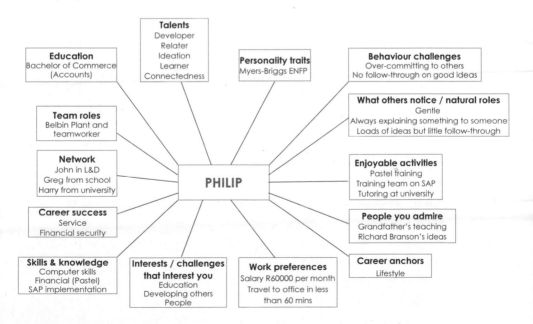

PULLING IT ALL TOGETHER

The initial reaction of many career navigators when they review their Self-Q tool results is relief that they do have strengths and can be of value. Many also say, 'Oh now I understand why I hate my current job.' This is all evidence of how most career-management strategies are failing people and serve only to damage their self-esteem, create desperation and instil fear.

Once you have done the hard work of completing the Self-Q tool, using the tips we give you in of this chapter, you can start to see a clearer picture of yourself and what you have to offer an employer or a team. It is like completing a puzzle – but without the box's lid to guide you to the final picture. It's best to start with the border, creating a framework, and then fill in the other pieces. At first you can't make out the picture but as you patiently insert more pieces, you can start to guess what it will be. And once all the pieces are in place, you see the picture in all its glory.

When you review your Self-Q tool, you are looking for interesting insights about yourself, your uniqueness, your challenges, your possibilities and most importantly, your career drivers. The Self-Q tool allows you to gather and synthesise the relevant information about you to enable your natural patterns and preferences to emerge. By looking inward before outward, you can become more aware of what your work preferences are, what interests you and what you have to offer an employer, a team or project (and even your family and friends).

Your insights may include a greater awareness and understanding of:

- The building blocks for your career (ie skills, knowledge, talents, interests and how they could work together to create a unique advantage);
- A trait, a talent or an interest that you had forgotten about or never knew you had;
- Work preferences or deal-breakers that are so important to you that you can't compromise on them;
- Patterns or connections (eg how your talents could be used to solve a problem you are interested in);
- How others' perception of you differs from how you see yourself;

- What comes naturally to you and where you can be at your best;
- Behaviour drivers;
- Gaps in your skills and knowledge that need to be rectified;
- How your behaviour challenges are holding you back from using all your strengths;
- Areas that you can develop into strengths and specialities;
- Aspects of yourself you have been ignoring or are in your blind spot;
- Possibilities for adding value to your company and role;
- Possibilities for what may be in line with your work preferences and career anchor;
- What you need to be engaged.

From these insights, you want to create a list of your career drivers, around which you will navigate your career. These questions may assist you in identifying your career drivers:

- How do I define career success?
- What am I doing when I am at my best? What talent am I using when I am most fulfilled and engaged?
- What do I really like about myself when I review the completed Self-Q tool?
- What do I really dislike about myself when I review the completed Self-Q tool?
- Are any of my work preferences non-negotiable?
- What are my unique advantages?
- How does my career anchor impact my career decisions?

Career drivers: What did Philip see?

Philip saw that he enjoyed sharing ideas, developing and relating to others and, when he thought about it, he did spend most of his waking hours 'explaining something to someone'. He saw his 'developer' pattern and he felt excited about finding a way to use it more.

He started to understand why he was full of ideas but did not follow through with them. He understood that he made decisions based on what he felt and why this frustrated his boss, who based her decisions on logical reasoning. He understood why he was always helping the members of his team and he saw the connection to his grandfather, who he admired.

He knew he had chosen to go into finance because the salaries were higher and he could see that he had tried to become someone he was not. He wondered aloud, 'What would my friends or my wife say if I changed my career now?'

He started to see more options for himself and even saw the beginnings of a purpose greater than himself. Yes, he saw hope and he welcomed it with open arms. He also felt fearful about making a career change at his stage of life. He said over and over again, 'I need to pay the bills. I have a family you know. I can't just change track as I need to pay for school fees and the house.'

Philip answered the career drivers questions as follows:

How do I define career success?
Providing for my family and creating a nest egg for the future.

What am I doing when I am at my best? What talent am I using when I am most fulfilled and engaged?
Developing and relating to others.

What do I really like about myself when I review the completed Self-Q tool?
I like to help others by teaching and explaining. I am intuitive and can relate well to others.

What do I really dislike about myself when I review the completed Self-Q tool?
I am not good at following through on my ideas.

Are any of my work preferences non-negotiable?
I want to spend time with my family and don't want to spend long times away from them.

What are my unique advantages?
People do approach me for help and most times I am able to explain things to them, especially financial package questions.

How does my career anchor impact my career decisions?
My career anchor is lifestyle which means that, to be engaged, I need to find and secure a work opportunity that will allow me to balance and integrate my personal needs with the requirements of my career.

Philip identified his career drivers as:
- Providing financially for his family;
- Using his 'developer' and 'relator' talents to explain and teach;
- Balancing his work with his family requirements;
- Partnering with someone or being in a team that would ensure he followed through on his ideas or would do the follow-through.

We are excited to say that, at the time of publishing this book, Philip is the head of training and development in a large IT company. It took time for him to develop the skills and knowledge needed to take on that role but he has shown that, with effort, it is possible to find a role that allows you to be more of who you are and be well paid.

ACCEPTANCE OF SELF

Everyone has preconceived ideas about what is good or bad. These ideas normally extend to many of the aspects covered in the Self-Q tool, such as personality traits, skills, education and work preferences. Many people fight against those parts of themselves that they have labelled as bad or that they would prefer to change. They focus their time and effort on changing what they have labelled as bad so that they can be more successful and wealthy, more liked, more what their parents hoped for, or more like other people they regard as 'successful'.

Everyone has a behaviour or two that, if changed, would result in improved relationships, work performance and maybe even overall happiness. These behaviours don't need to limit your or your team's progress or success: they can be improved through focused learning. You can also enhance your skills set, education and competencies to ensure that you remain relevant in the workplace.

It is also important to acknowledge that some aspects of yourself shown in the Self-Q tool just can't be changed no matter how much you try. These include some aspects of your talents and personality, what you enjoy and are drawn towards doing, who you admire and what roles you naturally play.

You have a choice. You can accept yourself and focus on becoming the best version of you, or you can try to be someone else and squash yourself into a different box. There is a fine line between wanting to improve yourself and wanting to change yourself.

The successful career navigator adopts the mindset of 'I seek to be engaged'. Adopting this mindset requires you to accept yourself and to put the majority of your energy into becoming more of the best you, and some energy into managing your limiting behaviours. More often we see career navigators trying to be people they are not in an effort to gain favour or finance. This is like trying to climb up a steep sand dune while others are walking on flat land. It takes so much more effort for them than for others with natural talent in that area and there is no guarantee that they will reach the top in time. Choose your challenges wisely by accepting to work with your strengths rather than fighting your weaknesses.

WHAT THIS MEANS FOR YOU

Identifying your career drivers allows you to see what you require in your career to be at your best and engaged. You have now looked inward and found what you need to know about yourself in order to move out into the world of work and find or create an opportunity that will allow you to be at your best and be engaged. This is the starting point for creating a competitive advantage.

You can expect your working understanding of self and your career drivers to evolve over time as you continue to ask the relevant questions and, through trial and error, find out what works for you as you become more effective at spotting the telltale signs.

COACHES' CORNER

Now it's your turn to complete the Self-Q tool. Download a Self-Q tool template from the website (www.navigatingyourcareer.com).

We have provided a little more detail about completing each block. As you do so, you need to keep in mind things you have done and things you'd like to do. In other words, you need to get a good balance between past and future while being honest and realistic in your assessments.

For many of the blocks, we have suggested a formal assessment or test. If you have done the recommended assessment at some stage in the past, or something similar to it, insert the results. If you are struggling to complete the block, doing the test may assist you in gaining more insight into yourself. Some tests do cost money to do so we have tried to suggest only free or cheap tests that should be accessible to you.

It is also perfectly fine to complete the blocks based on your own self-assessment (this is actually our preferred approach). One reason for this is that the tests often define who you have been, rather than who you want to be; they look at what you've done, rather than what you'd like to do.

You may want to ask a number of other people for help, including family, friends, colleagues and bosses. The more confident you are that these people will be truthful, the better the results will be.

As you saw with Philip's example, you don't have to complete all the blocks in order but you do have to complete them all by the end. It might take some time to do this, and we highly recommend that you stop reading this book until you have completed most of the blocks, even if it takes a few days or weeks to do properly.

Block 1: Education

List any formal learning that you have completed, as well as any qualifications you have.

Block 2: Talents

List your natural patterns of thought, feeling and behaviour. For example, you may naturally show empathy towards others or you may be naturally competitive (as opposed to cooperative) and quickly see all the ways to win. Talents are often difficult to identify, as you probably think that these talents are just natural. You probably think everybody thinks or acts in these ways.

We suggest taking the StrengthsFinder 2.0 test from the Gallup Organisation and the StandOut test from Marcus Buckingham. These tests can be found in the books by the same names, or at the websites associated with those books.

Block 3: Personality traits

Identify the personality traits that may impact your career. For example, you may be extroverted and gain energy from being with other people. Many of these personality profiling systems also suggest a variety of suitable jobs or careers. You may want to include these on your Self-Q tool as a reminder of the recommendation. Remember, however, that your career decisions need to be based on all your career drivers (one of which may be personality) and not on your personality alone. We suggest taking any of the following tests:

- DISC personality profiling (www.discusonline.com).
- EvaleX (www.evalex.com).
- Enneagram of personality (www.enneagraminstitute.com).
- Myers-Briggs Type Indicator® (www.myersbriggs.org). The Myers-Briggs Type Indicator® (MBTI®) personality inventory is to make the theory of psychological types described by C G Jung understandable and useful in people's lives. It looks at four different factors of personality: where you get your energy from (introvert or extrovert), how you prefer to take in information (sensing or intuition), how you prefer to make decisions (thinking or feeling), and how you prefer to relate to the external world (judging or perceiving).

Block 4: Behaviour challenges

Identify the behaviours or traits that hold you back from being your best. Identify those behaviours that frustrate those around you or reduce your own effectiveness. You may be conscious of these behaviours or traits or they may be in your blind spot and you will need the help of others to identify them.

For example, you may be good at beginning a project but notice that you don't always complete what you start. You procrastinate or have poor time management. You may blame everyone around when you are under pressure or take all the credit when a project is a success.

Block 5: What others notice and your natural roles

Ask others what they notice about you. What role do you naturally play? What are you known for? For example, you may naturally connect with everyone in the office and are always the first to accept party invitations. You may spend your time helping everyone around you. You may be very competitive and always want to win. You may be able to influence the others' behaviour. You may organise all social events.

Block 6: Activities you enjoy and your successes

Identify the activities that you enjoy in your current job. Identify the preferred activities in your previous job. Identify your successes. For example, you enjoyed solving a client problem, you enjoyed coming up with new ideas; you enjoyed analysing a problem or organising a party.

Block 7: Traits or accomplishments of people you admire

Think of a person you admire. Identify the traits or accomplishments that impressed you. This means that you perceive this to be worthwhile or important and it is likely that this is what you aspire to. As an example, you may admire a teacher who cared about each and every child in the class and adjusted his teachings to suit each person. Therefore, it is likely that you value inclusion and will strive for this yourself.

Block 8: Career anchors

Your career anchor is what you would not give up if you were faced with a career decision. For example, you may desire autonomy and independence and would not be able to give this up to work for a corporate.

We suggest taking the Career Anchors Self-Assessment, developed by Edgar Schein (www.careeranchorsonline.com).

Block 9: Work preferences

Your work preferences include salary and benefit requirements, work hours and flexibility, travel (both to work and for work), and company and people requirements. You may also want to consider whether growth opportunities are important to you or not. Are you looking for creative work as opposed to routine? How much autonomy do you prefer? You need to identify the elements that are dealbreakers and on which you would not be prepared to compromise. For example, you may not want to work for less than a certain amount per month, or you may not want to drive more than 20 km to work.

Block 10: Interests or challenges that interest you

Notice what you enjoy reading or speaking about, and what problems you would be keen to spend time and energy solving. For example, you may be interested in developing people. You may be interested in protecting the environment. You may be interested in energy-saving devices.

We suggest taking either of the following tests:

- Self-Directed Search, originally created by John Holland (www.self-directed-search.com).
- Jackson Vocational Interest Survey (www.jvis.com).

Block 11: Skills and knowledge

Identify what you are able to do, what you know and what you have done in previous jobs. You may want to do a self-assessment of your skills level, as Philip did for his computer skills. This would be the list of skills you'd typically include in a résumé. For example, you may include skills like: managing client relationships, managing computer servers, completing bank reconciliations, using Microsoft Excel.

Block 12: Career success

Every person has an idea of success. It may be financial success, recognition, having certain skills, or achieving balance in life. You need to identify what you want from your career. For example, you may want to sell your business for a profit or be able to balance your work and family time.

Block 13: Network

Identify people who can assist you with achieving career success. For example, you could approach your MBA study group – most of whom have taken senior positions in corporate companies – or your father's best friend, who is the head of an IT company.

Block 14: Team roles

Identify the role you play in a team and what you can be relied upon to do. For example, you may be great with ideas in team meetings but hopeless at following through on those ideas. You may be the mediator in the group when conflict arises.

We suggest taking the Belbin Team Roles test (www.belbin.com) to identify the role you play in a team.

Other tests

You may feel you want to spend a little bit of money to complete some of the more complex tests and include the results in the Self-Q tool – but in most cases, that is unnecessary. These include but are not limited to: *Career Navigator*, an online career guidance process designed by Dirk Visser; *Solutionsfinding*, a brain profiling instrument designed by Kobus Neethling; and *CareerStorm Navigator*, another online tool for leadership and career development. Dean Sutic has also created the *Work Atlas*, which overlays various psychometric tests to identify a career navigator's values, interests and personality.

Each of these tools focuses attention on a particular aspect or aspects of who you are and the results can be included in the Self-Q tool.

MAIN POINTS

You need a working understanding of self to identify your career drivers for effective career navigation. The Self-Q tool provides a framework for gathering relevant information about yourself for career navigation.

You can expect your working understanding of self to evolve over time as you continue to ask the relevant questions and, through trial and error, find out what works for you as you become more effective at spotting the telltale signs.

The example of Philip, when combined with many other similar stories, teaches us the very thing we need to know about career dilemmas: There is a path out of a career dilemma and it starts by obtaining a working self-understanding.

SUGGESTED READING

StrengthsFinder 2.0 by Tom Rath (Gallup Press, 2007)
Now Discover Your Strengths by Marcus Buckingham (The Free Press, 2001)
Career Anchors by Edgar H Schein (John Wiley & Sons, 2006)
Mojo by Marshall Goldsmith (Profile Books, 2010) for managing limiting
    behaviours
Gifts Differing: Understanding Personality Type by Isabel Briggs Myers (CPP, 1980)
    for more understanding of Myers-Briggs Personality Type Indicator
Management Teams: Why They Succeed or Fail by R Meredith Belbin (Elsevier,
    2010) for more understanding of team roles

A BIT OF INSPIRATION

'If you wish to achieve worthwhile things in your personal and career life, you
must become a worthwhile person in your own self-development.'
Brian Tracy, one of the world's most famous life coaches

4

STAGE 2: UNDERSTANDING THE NEW WORLD OF WORK

'All we have to decide is what to do with the time that is given us.'
Gandalf in J R R Tolkien's The Lord of the Rings: The Fellowship of the Ring

'The secret of success in life is for a man to be
ready for his opportunity when it comes.'
Benjamin Disraeli

Now that you have a clearer idea of who you are and what type of work will bring out the best *you*, you need to turn your attention outward and gain an understanding of what the world of work in the 21st century looks like. This is Stage 2 of the Career Navigation Model and is potentially the most difficult. Most people don't even realise how much they don't know about the job market and the many different career options there are, both now and in the future.

Because of this, the default advice that most people receive from concerned parents or school guidance counsellors is to become as educated as possible and preferably become a lawyer, doctor, engineer, accountant, actuary, architect or some similarly well-paid professional. Many young women are given options that include becoming a nurse, secretary or teacher – in many male-dominated parts of the world, these are still considered the best options for women. Some people are given very little advice at all, as their parents may not have enough work experience. All in all, this type of advice bears little resemblance to the actual world of work.

Knowing what your options are is of vital importance. What does your set of skills, talents, interests, experiences and all the other Self-Q tool factors actually equip you to do? And does such a job exist?

This book obviously cannot give you all the information you need in order to understand the world of work and choose a specific job. What we will help you to do is understand some of the shifts that are taking place in the world of work so you can plot a landscape for yourself. After all, this is the world in which you will spend the rest of your career.

But first there's good news and there's bad news.

The good news is that there have never been as many opportunities as there are now for you to create your perfect career. Traditional jobs still exist, but more and more companies are looking for a different type of specialised worker. We are also about to experience an unprecedented number of smaller start-up companies that will be looking for a wide range of people with many different types of skills and backgrounds. The only requirements, in many cases, will be passion, a willingness to work hard and learn as you go, combined with a can-do attitude. Just reading this book means you probably have most of these already!

What is even more exciting is that it is becoming more and more likely that your unique set of characteristics will find a place in the world of work. To put it another way: you don't have to endure a job you don't like; you can find the perfect type of work for you. This truly is an age of possibility and opportunity.

However, in the aftermath of the 2008 financial crisis and the years of economic downturn that have followed, we are facing probably the toughest job market in living memory. There are also other factors, besides the economy, that are making this situation even worse – and these factors are going to last much longer than the financial crisis. You can't wait them out! We look at them in depth in this chapter, and we're sure you'll agree with us that the world of work is about to change dramatically. It will change in such a way that there will be fewer workers and work will be harder to find.

This can all be quite depressing but there is hope. The new world of work is not going to be more of the same. As the second decade of the 21st century unfolds, it's going to be increasingly obvious that work as we know it is changing quickly and substantially. Some people are going to be caught out by this, and that will be bad news for them, but others (like you!) are going to put the effort in to work on their careers, get ahead of the changes that are coming and seize the opportunities that are emerging.

So let's paint you a picture of what's changing (and what isn't). And why.

THE OLD WORLD OF WORK

The working world that most people consider to be 'normal' today is only just over 100 years old. When the Industrial Revolution (or 'machine age') began, it became clear that the skills, attitudes and lifestyle patterns of a largely agricultural society were not adequate for the new world of factories, cities and machines.

Schools were therefore carefully and thoughtfully redesigned, not only to provide children with the knowledge needed for this new world, but also to socialise them into the new work pattern as well. School buildings were built to look like factories; classes were laid out with work benches in neat rows (just like the factories), and children were required to be quiet and obey instructions given by their 'supervisor', the teacher. The content that children were taught was broken down into neat little units called subjects and children were encouraged to specialise in whichever of these subjects they showed some aptitude. This pattern continued all the way through colleges and universities until out the other side emerged either factory labourers or white-collar workers who worked in the cubicle 'factories' of the world's offices.

We're generalising, we know. We also know that, for some people, this type of work life is quite fulfilling. It hasn't been all bad. It did, after all, create the world as we know it today. For many people, this is still the model of work they have in their minds and still frames their thinking about their jobs and their career prospects. This model is constantly reinforced by parents, by schools, by large corporate companies or government departments, and by old-school bosses and managers who abound in those organisations.

So, for example, in Chapter 1 we saw that Kagiso, the son of a miner and domestic worker, was making his way through a graduate programme at a bank. Like many people around the world, Kagiso's network of family and friends has little experience of the world of work he found himself in, yet it is this network to which people like Kagiso usually turn to ask for career advice. With little understanding of the old world of work, let alone the newly emerging one, the advice that Kagiso had received was confusing, irrelevant and, in some cases, even damaging to his career. This is also true for people in family businesses or those who follow their parents into similar jobs.

Graeme remembers distinctly a conversation he had with his father back in the 1980s when he was a teenager. We are sure you had a very similar conversation with your parents. 'Dad, what should I be when I grow up?' This is more than a question about career choices or job options; this is a question about security, about personality and about the way the world of work is structured. It's a question every young generation asks its parents.

The answer that most young people were given when Graeme's father was a child (about half a century ago) was to get a good job in a big company and stay there. Security was found at the large corporates and at state-run organisations that promised cradle-to-grave employment with a very structured and slowly progressive career path through multiple layers of management and leadership.

By the time Graeme asked this question in the 1980s, the world had begun to shift. Graeme was told, 'Become a professional.' Security and good job prospects belonged to those who were custodians of the information at the heart of the 'information economy'; in other words, the group of jobs we call 'professions': lawyers, doctors, engineers, accountants, actuaries, architects, vets, psychologists and teachers, to name the most popular. In essence, this class of worker charges out its brain power by the hour and, over the last few decades, it has been exceptionally good advice to enter one of these professions, if at all possible.

But now that the Internet makes data and information freely available to everyone, everywhere, all the time, the days when specialist knowledge gave you an edge are nearly over. It's our view that these professions, and the process of becoming and staying a professional, represent the pinnacle of the old way of working.

The problem for Kagiso, and many others working their way up through big companies these days, is that the rules have changed substantially. It used to be the case that, if you delivered what was asked of you, and stayed around long enough, you'd be guaranteed a promotion up through the ranks. A career just looked after itself and the human resources team was there to smooth the way for you. This is what Kagiso was hoping would happen but, like many others,

Kagiso was finding that this isn't the way it works these days. The old rules don't apply anymore.

NEW RULES

Over the past two decades the role of the HR department in most companies has shifted dramatically from being responsible for managing the personal development of internal staff to becoming the gatekeeper for recruitment. At a recent conference, Graeme heard an HR expert say, 'HR's job now is to hire and fire, and make sure the company doesn't get sued for it.' That might be a bit cynical, but one thing is sure: in most organisations, HR no longer manages the career paths of individuals. To put it plainly, HR is not there for you.

Another new rule is that age and experience are no longer indicators of success. There are no guarantees that doing everything that is asked of you will get you a promotion. In fact, you might even lose your job. Employers often complain about the lack of loyalty from a younger generation who move jobs and companies regularly. In reality, this lack of loyalty was started by the companies themselves, as they have responded to the last few economic downturns by retrenching staff in large numbers, while often paying their CEOs huge bonuses.

There are many other new rules and we'll look at a few below, but our point is simple: it's natural that Kagiso's generation feels that the world of work they've entered is broken. In fact, it's not broken; it's just changing. Dramatically. And forever.

A NEW WORLD OF WORK IS EMERGING

One of the pioneers of a new approach to work is Seth Godin, who is probably best known as a marketing expert, but really is a guru of the new world of work. In an interview on 12 January 2012 (see www.businessinsider.com), he summed up what we're trying to say:

> The way we do business is changing fast and in order to keep up, your entire mentality about work has to change just as quickly. Unfortunately, most

people aren't adapting fast enough to this change in the workplace. For 80 years, you got a job, you did what you were told and you retired ... But the days when people were able to get above-average pay for average work are over. If you're the average person out there doing average work, there's going to be someone else out there doing the exact same thing as you, but cheaper. Now that the industrial economy is over, you should forget about doing things just because it's assigned to you, or you'll be racing to the bottom.

A new world of work is emerging and there are at least five key forces driving the changes we're experiencing. By understanding these forces, you'll be more equipped to know where your best contribution will be, and be powerfully in action as you consider your future career options.

Technology

The first and most obvious driver of change is technology. The advent of the personal computer and the Internet, together with the continual and rapid increase in the processing speed, storage capacity and communication bandwidth between computers, have meant that many tasks that might have been fulfilled by people in the past are now being done by computers.

Imagine approaching a wheat farmer 100 years ago and telling him that he'd soon be able to get rid of all the farm labourers (even the extra labourers he employed during harvesting season) and replace them all with a single person and a machine. The machine would be able to drive up and down the wheat fields, harvesting the wheat, stripping out the good bits from the bad, sorting everything for him and packaging it for delivery to the marketplace. The farmer would have laughed, of course. Impossible. Through his laughter, he would have said, 'What do you know? You don't know my business. That could never happen.'

But of course it did. The machine was a combine harvester, and there were other machines, too. That technology caused the number of workers needed on farms to be dramatically reduced.

Imagine we had approached a factory manager 50 years ago and said something very similar. Imagine we had said, 'In just a few years' time, all your current factory workers will be replaced by machines. These machines will be able to do the most sophisticated physical tasks, including precise spot-welding and the putting together of very finely integrated pieces. They will be able to identify defects, do their own quality control and package everything for delivery to your marketplace.'

The factory manager would no doubt have laughed at us. Between his chuckling he would have said, 'What do you know about my work? That could never happen.'

But of course that is precisely what happened. We call those machines robots, and factories are now computerised and automated.

So now, when we consider what technology can do to our current world of work, we have to take seriously the potential for computers to replace professionals. It is fairly obvious that those people whose main task is thinking, communication, or data processing and analysis are in danger from these 21st century machines.

As we head into the second decade of the 21st century, we are on the brink of a data revolution in our businesses. The age of *big data* is about to break on us. For example, Tesco, the largest supermarket chain in the United Kingdom, collects 1.5 billion pieces of data every month. These come from smart RFID tags in all their goods, from surveillance videos, from clock-in details of staff, from the purchasing details and credit card usage of all their customers, and from Tesco's online store, where not only what people buy is recorded but also what people search for and then *don't* buy. Where possible, all of this information is connected to individuals and to specific stores. The data is then analysed on an ongoing basis and used dynamically to manage stock control at individual stores; to change the relative positioning of products in the stores; to deal with staffing requirements in various regions of the country, and even to create completely customised brochures that get sent out to consumers throughout the UK. When you receive a Tesco brochure in the mail you can almost be certain that it has been entirely customised for you and that you are the only person receiving that particular brochure.

How do you analyse that amount of data? You can't put 1.5 billion pieces of data into an Excel spreadsheet! The answer is by using computer processing power. It's this level of data analysis that is going to be where computers come to the fore in the world of work.

This level of computing power is affecting the job prospects of some highly skilled and highly paid professionals, such as stockbrokers and traders. Computer programmes can now do their jobs much better by reducing human errors, speeding up the time taken to do a transaction, and accurately anticipating market changes faster than a human can. (Of course, every dark cloud has a silver lining: there are many, many more jobs for the people who can write the programmes and support the hardware required to implement these computerised systems.)

And, then, in the last few years, we have seen the emergence of a new use for computers. It's generally called social media and refers to the way in which people now use computers, smartphones and tablet devices to stay almost permanently connected with each other and the world. Some people still struggle to see the benefit of all the chatter that happens in social media but it's clear that this is more than just a fad or a teenage toy. Social media is changing how we use technology to engage with other people and it will be a driving force of change in the way we work, the way we interact with others, and the way things are bought and sold in the future.

So computers have slowly been taking over and redefining the jobs and functions of labourers, factory workers and now, increasingly, middle managers, white-collar workers and professionals. Technology is a driver of change in the new world of work and it cannot be ignored.

Those professionals who wish to ensure that they cannot be replaced by computers need to develop skills that transcend mere information processing. They need to be truly global in their mindsets, lift their understanding above the ordinary, be creative and operate at a level their colleagues cannot. We'll return to these thoughts in Chapter 7.

How long will you work?

There used to be a very clear career trajectory for people. About 15 years of studying; then about five years doing an apprenticeship or 'learning the ropes' somewhere; then working your way up to, and through middle management; followed by a certain number of years of leadership within an organisation, and finally retirement and a few years enjoying the fruits of your labour before it was all over. Most people's mental picture of that trajectory is designed around a 70-year lifespan.

The problem is that we're living a good two decades longer than that. In many instances, people have simply believed that they could extend the retirement years, and be in a non-working situation for three or four decades. In 2011, numerous marches and strikes began around the world as many government workers objected to attempts to increase the retirement age. These will fail. It is physically, psychologically and, possibly even spiritually unhealthy to spend 30 years working, and then 30 years not working. Human beings are not built for that.

Other factors aside, though, it's mainly a financial issue. We cannot afford to retire as we do now. This is becoming increasingly apparent around the world. Governments are waking up to the fact that they do not have the resources to be able to provide the level of benefits and retirement options that they have promised their populations. The same is true of private pensions and insurance. The whole system is outdated. Today's 20-somethings will not be able to retire as their grandparents did.

We need to readjust our mindset about how many years we spend in each part of our careers. Many people are opting to study longer, with an increasing emphasis on postgraduate and specialist qualifications. Many people are taking more time in their 20s and 30s to move around between different career options before settling down and choosing one that they wish to focus on and progress in. Many are choosing to make radical mid-career moves (like Philip). Others are choosing to delay retirement, or to start new businesses or careers in their twilight years. Each of these options – and many others besides – is becoming increasingly acceptable.

Engaging with difference

The third driving force of change is one that has possibly been happening even longer than the technology and work pattern shifts discussed above, and that is the increasingly diverse worldviews that people have in today's workplace.

When we talk about diversity, some people roll their eyes – they've been on one too many diversity training programmes, trying to sensitise them to the needs of women, other races and religions, or some other minority group. We mean something bigger than this. By 'diversity', we mean the different worldviews that people have: different expectations, different views of what 'normal' is and different preferences. The world of work has never had to deal with as many differing worldviews as it does today.

By way of example, let's consider the increasing role of women in the world of work. From the feminist revolutions of the 1960s and 70s, women have been working to bring equality into the workplace, and in many countries around the world, there are now more women officially employed in the workplace than men. In many countries, there are also more women at university than men.

Of course this doesn't tell the whole story. Women are still grossly under-represented at senior leadership levels. But what is happening, and will continue to happen over the next few years, is not just that we get more women bodies into the workplace, but that we increasingly get a feminine *influence* in the workplace. One of the most significant implications of a more feminine influence in the workplace is the growing emphasis on work-life integration; the rising demand for both maternity and paternity leave, and a different approach to leadership, management and strategic decision-making. For example, we have heard many people argue that the 2008 financial crisis might not have happened if there were more women in leadership at the world's banks. These types of comments are impossible to verify, of course, but they do point to a shift in our thinking about the importance of different points of view in the workplace.

We could consider similar examples involving religion, culture, ethnicity or sexual orientation and different worldviews would emerge. Each would make the same points: we're dealing with more difference than we have ever done before and, if we're prepared to embrace these different worldviews, we will produce teams and organisations that are more resilient, more innovative and probably healthier too.

Globalisation

A fourth driver of change in the world of work is globalisation. Arguably the most powerful entities in the world at the moment are multinational corporations, many of which earn more money than most of the world's countries and have more power than many of the world's governments. These multinationals have made it possible for people to travel around the world and experience more diversity than any previous generations have ever experienced. As we just discussed, this brings additional stresses and requirements for people who, on a day-to-day basis, have to deal with others who have different work styles. This has produced a level of complexity which was previously unknown at the lower levels of the organisation.

Globalisation has also been responsible for driving other changes in the world of work. People are less bound to office hours now, as they may report to someone in Hong Kong and a colleague in São Paulo may request information from them a moment later. People are also competing with everyone everywhere for the work they're offering their companies.

In a number of his books and columns, award-winning journalist, Thomas Friedman has made the point that the only jobs that will never be under threat in a 'flat world' are those that are truly local and those that are truly global. No matter how rich and powerful you are, or how many frequent flier miles you earn each year, when your toilet won't flush, the only person you want to see is a local plumber. You feel a similar way towards the person who delivers the parcel you ordered from the other side of the world. Conceivably, your fitness trainer, GP or tax consultant could actually live anywhere and provide advice and assistance digitally, but most people still prefer these types of encounters to be in the 'real' world with real people who they can actually meet with.

'I live to work' becomes 'I work to live'

The final trend to consider as a driving force for change in the world of work is a generational shift in the value placed on work itself. The baby boomer generation, who were born in the 1950s and 60s, were the last generation for who work was a priority over all other aspects of life. Back in the 1970s and 80s, when these young people were offered promotions, they would often accept a move to a different city or a different region without even consulting their spouses or families. They would simply arrive home with the 'good news' that they had been promoted and the family would be moving. That would be unheard of for today's young people, who prioritise family before work and put their own personal health before their boss's demands.

It has been said that the older generations lived to work and that the younger generations now work so that they can have a life. It can also be said that previous generations might even be prepared to do anything and everything for their companies. Today's young people are not lazy – they are prepared to work hard, but only if they are achieving *their* goals while working. If that goal is to rise up through the ranks in a company and become a senior leader in an organisation, they may well be prepared to be workaholics, putting in 18-hour days, seven days a week. But if they are simply working in a company to get that company's name on their résumé and they plan to move on or even take a gap year or shift professions, they may very well decline to work overtime and only put in the minimum effort required to be vaguely acceptable in their boss's eyes.

This is a hugely significant shift in values within the world of work and is still a mystery to many older leaders within organisations.

WHAT THE NEW WORLD OF WORK WILL LOOK LIKE

These five forces are merely a sampling of some of the trends that are changing the world of work. We selected these as they represent the most disruptive, obvious forces, but all you need to do is watch the news channels every evening to see some of the other forces we could have mentioned: the scarcity of natural resources; the volatility of global financial markets; changing legislation and regulations; urbanisation and migration; the growing middle class in emerging countries, and so many more.

Our goal was not to write a book about the future (see the reading list at the end of the chapter if you'd like to read further on this), but rather to get you thinking about how *your* world of work is about to change.

We will come back to the types of skills you'll need to stay ahead of the pack (see Chapter 7), but for now, we want to highlight some of the key ways in which we believe this new world of work will develop. As you read these predictions, keep your Self-Q tool next to you and notice where you have areas of strength or weakness in relation to these characteristics. The people who are likely to be most successful in the years ahead will be those who are best equipped to work in the ways we outline overleaf. How ready are *you* for this new world of work?

'Always on'

The days of working nine to five and having weekends completely off are long gone. Employers give their staff smartphones and tablet computers for a reason: they want them working all the time and to be accessible 24/7. Very few people nowadays have a strict divide between work and non-work life, and it's taking its toll: most people haven't yet learnt how to live and work in this always-on, always-accessible world. Checking emails on holiday, sending text messages to colleagues at the weekend, and not thinking of either of these as overtime, is the new normal.

Work-life integration

Having said that, though, the freedom that the mobile digital world has given people has been gratefully accepted, especially by the younger generation. Maybe because young people watched their parents work their lives away, the workplace's newest employees want time to develop their personal lives and interests outside of work. They also want work itself to be more fulfilling – not just a paycheck and a survival existence. It's not about balance between work and non-work; it's about integrating these two aspects intp a seamless whole.

In fact, many younger people would put family and friends before work if they were really pushed. Smart employers understand this and are adjusting incentives and expectations. In most cases, by providing flexibility, they get more out of their staff than if they held them to stricter office hours.

Flexiblity

Because the workplace has gone digital, staff do not need to be based in an office and can often take their work on the road. This provides opportunities to live closer to family; take a few hours out of the office for personal activities while still remaining connected; relocate to a new city or country; travel, or simply work from home more often.

Flexibility is also reflected in how companies treat their employees, and the terms and conditions of that employment. Most companies now have a lot more personalisation and flexibility when dealing with individuals who work for them.

Speed

The speed at which things need to be done can be quite staggering. Email and text messages have speeded up expected response times dramatically, and the increasing use of instant messaging (IM) over the next few years will serve only to make things feel even more immediate than they do now. Smartphones and tablet computers will be ever present, and our instant response to these insistent devices will be required. Although speed and efficiency are not the same things, speed is often valued in, and of itself, in the new world of work.

Complexity and constant change

The world of work's level of complexity and the speed at which things change are now relentless. This requires a level of understanding, with strategic insights and skills sets that, even 10 years ago, were only needed at senior levels of organisations. Today, these are required throughout the organisation, right down to the front line. Everyone is required to think and act strategically as never before. This is one of the key defining points of the new world of work.

Unlearning and relearning

In the new world of work it's not enough to be learning. You have to learn new things every month just to stand still. Now more than ever, Alvin Toffler's famous quote in his 1970 bestseller *Future Shock* is true. When looking forward to the world of today, he said, 'The illiterate of the 21st century will not be those that cannot read or write, but those that cannot learn, unlearn, relearn.' We need to learn how to unlearn bad habits and attitudes, and destructive patterns and frameworks.

Personal branding

Tom Peters was right – the 21st century is about 'Brand You'. Online branding is easy and cheap: start your own blog; get a Facebook page or Twitter account; promote yourself on LinkedIn, or even get your own website. Making a name for yourself is smarter than ever in this turbulent economy and it increases the chance that someone who knows of you will come to you with a job, rather than you having to look for one.

Smaller, self-directed, virtual teams

Working with colleagues in remote locations and across multiple time zones is becoming the norm. These teams are often without formal management structures, and operate virtually. Some members of these teams are also temporary and brought in on a project basis, using resources sourced from websites like www.elance.com. Maybe you can offer your services through this system.

Smaller companies and entrepreneurs

Whether it's because they're out of work or just unhappy with their current jobs, 20-somethings are about to lead an entrepreneurial charge. And they'll be joined by their boomer grandparents, who are going to refuse to retire. Enabled by the technology that has removed the traditional barriers to starting a business, young and old will turn hobbies into companies, provide services for local people and seize countless opportunities that are available for small businesses in every community. As a career navigator, starting your own business should always be on your list of possibilities.

Opportunity

We hope you get the sense that we're excited about this new world of work. Although the headline news is that there will be fewer jobs, we believe that there are many more opportunities than ever before for dedicated, hard-working career navigators.

Remember Tanya, the nurse who was considering changing her career completely? Her story is typical of many professionals, who have followed all the 'correct' career paths. Like Tanya, they may even have done this very well and be earning both praise and promotions. Yet they feel unfulfilled and empty inside.

The new world of work is the perfect place for them, as it provides them with any number of alternative options. Tanya considered becoming an entrepreneur and starting her own business providing art therapy. She thought she could contract to the hospital to provide art therapy for patients as they recuperate. She could open a post-operative care facility. She could join a post-operative centre on a flexible basis while she obtained business and management skills, with her eye on becoming a hospital manager. She could join a team of medical professionals as they provided services abroad for a limited period.

For Tanya, taking the step out of full-time employment felt too big a first step, so we also counselled her to start the journey by using her free time to develop skills, experience and contacts that might eventually lead to her dream of an art therapy centre. Sometimes big career moves can be made in small steps, as long as you don't lose sight of the final goal destination.

WHAT'S IN IT FOR YOU?

If this is the new world of work, then what does it all mean for you? As we said, we're excited about it for a number of reasons.

Firstly, it's easier than ever for you to find and access people you don't know, who might be useful for your career navigation. You no longer have to find ways to meet a company's CEO at an expensive fundraising event to get attention. Instead, you can Tweet, link to a blog, tag in Facebook, send an email, or use any other digital connections in order to get someone (especially a recruiter) to notice you. This type of targeted networking is becoming more and more important for career navigators.

Secondly, it is now acceptable to have multiple jobs and to go job-hopping. In the new world of work, you can switch jobs as often as you want, as long as each move continues to help you learn and grow (and you can explain to a recruiter who's checking your résumé how each move did that). If a job isn't working for you, find another. No future employer will judge you for jumping ship after a year if a better opportunity came along, especially if you show you were proactive for going after that opportunity. Employers like go-getters.

Thirdly, it's never too late (or too early) to make a change. Making a choice of subjects in the middle of your teenage years does not set you on a path through your studies and into a career that cannot be changed. Even in retirement, the new world of work understands – even expects – you to be adapting, changing and trying something new.

Full-time jobs aren't the only option. The term 'portfolio career' was first coined by Charles Handy in his book *The Age of Unreason* (Random House, 2002). Having a portfolio career involves pursuing a number of different jobs, usually simultaneously, on a part-time or shared-time basis. Even if being an entrepreneur isn't for you, don't assume you have to get a day job just because everyone you know has one. That's old-world-of-work thinking. And don't forget that digital tools now make all of this both easier and cheaper for you to do than ever before.

This new world of work is exciting because it is now more possible than ever before to make a living doing work you love.

COACHES' CORNER

As you consider each of the drivers of change in the new world of work, there are key career questions to ask yourself:

- How computer literate are you? How 'connected' are you? Do you have social media profiles and how are you managing them?
- How long do you think you're going to live for? We know this is a wild question to ask and that you can't know for sure. But think about it. If modern medicine, medical robotics and genetic science could extend your life, and you could live to 200 years old, would you want to? If you could live reasonably healthily to 100, would you want to? What would each decade between now and then be like for you? Can you afford to retire? Do you want to?
- One of the key skills needed by any worker or leader in the new world of work is to have a 'global mindset'. This is the ability to see the world through other people's eyes, to accept easily that your way is not necessarily the right way or the only way, and the ability to appreciate difference. On a scale of one to 10, how would you rate your own global mindset? Now, more importantly, how do you know your rating is accurate? Specifically, what have you done recently to challenge and expand your own worldview?
- How can you extend what you do and who you are to be either truly local or truly global?
- Where do your priorities lie? Consider this quote by Seth Godin from *Do Less – ChangeThis Manifesto*:

If your goal is to be big, there's no doubt that taking every gig you can makes sense. Pricing for the masses, building the biggest factory and running as fast as you can is the very best way to get big. And if big equals successful, you're done. Many of us have realized, though, that big doesn't equal successful. If success (for you) is a decent (or indecent) wage plus the time to do really good work and enjoy both your job and your family, then perhaps you're trying too hard and doing too much. Perhaps you need to be a lot pickier in what you do and for who you do it.

- What disruptive forces do you think are most significant in your industry and for your career?

MAIN POINTS

The world of work is changing rapidly and you need to be informed about the current trends and opportunities and those that are likely to exist in the coming years.

Five key forces are driving the emergence of a new world of work. These are technology, demographics, diversity, globalisation and generational values shifts. The new world of work has different rules for success and failure, and different structures and rhythms. It is also filled with opportunity for those willing to adapt to new styles of working.

You want to know what other navigators and players are doing in the world of work and the plans they are making to maximise their opportunities in the future world of work. Being aware of emerging trends and opportunities does not mean constantly looking for a career change. Rather, it means looking for the ways of making whatever career you choose maximally successful.

SUGGESTED READING

Karaoke Capitalism by Kjell Nordström and Jonas Ridderstråle (Financial Times/Prentice Hall, 2004)

Linchpin: Are You Indispensable? by Seth Godin (Piatkus Books, 2010)

Re-Imagine! Business Excellence in a Disruptive Age by Tom Peters (Dorling Kindersley, 2009)

The Future of Management by Gary Hamel (Harvard Business School Press, 2007)

The Cluetrain Manifesto by Rick Levine, Christopher Locke, David Searls and David Weinberger (Basic Books, 2001)

The Shift: The Future of Work is Already Here by Lynda Gratton (Collins, 2011)

5

STAGE 3: CREATING POSSIBILITIES

'Let your mind start a journey thru a strange new world.
Leave all thoughts of the world you knew before.
Let your soul take you where you long to be ...
Close your eyes let your spirit start to soar, and you'll live as you've never
lived before.'
Erich Fromm

'Effective people are not problem-minded; they're opportunity-minded.
They feed opportunities and starve problems.'
Stephen Covey

NEW POSSIBILITIES

When you are trapped, your vision is limited to what is around you. You don't see, or you just *can't* see, what lies beyond The Trap. At first, you fight The Trap and when you are tired of fighting, you develop ways to cope. You start to pray that you will win the lottery or someone will help you, so you can escape this career and do something that you love. Or you work harder and harder at something you don't want to be doing, hoping that somehow a breakthrough will happen and you can leave it all behind.

That's why Stage 3 of the Career Navigation Model is to look up and out – beyond the horizon.

There is an old story, retold by many different people in many different ways. A shoe factory sends two sales people to an African region to study prospects for expanding their footwear business. One sends back a message that says, 'Situation hopeless. Nobody wears shoes.'

The other reports back triumphantly, 'Amazing business opportunity! Nobody owns shoes!'

One person sees no shoes, and all evidence points to hopelessness. To another person, the same conditions point to abundance and possibility.

Do you see possibilities or is your thinking limited to what is considered a reasonable or safe option?

So often, people don't extend their thinking to what may be possible. They don't consider all the short- and long-term possibilities, and how they can combine their talents, skills and knowledge in differing environments to achieve different goals. They even believe some of their negative thoughts. They limit their futures by using past experiences as constraints on what is possible.

As a career navigator, you need to understand what your past experiences are and consciously leave them in the past to create a clearing for the future. Only then will you be able to consider all the possibilities and create a different future.

You Can If You Think You Can!

If you think you are beaten, you are.
If you think you dare not, you don't.
If you like to win, but you think you can't,
It is almost certain you won't.

If you think you'll lose, you're lost,
For out in the world we find
Success begins with a fellow's will.
It's all in the state of mind.

If you think you are outclassed, you are.
You've got to think high to rise.
You've got to be sure of yourself before
You can ever win a prize.

Life's battles don't always go
To the stronger or faster man.
But soon or late the man who wins
Is the man who thinks he can.

C W Longenecker

Stop for a moment to think about this a little more. Your career dilemma may be caused by your own thinking (or lack of thinking). Maybe your circumstances are not to blame. Perhaps your limited view of yourself and your possibilities is holding you back.

Part of achieving career success and fulfilment is directing your thoughts to change your future and your feelings about the future. You want to take on a director's role in your brain and no longer be the slave to your limiting and negative thoughts. You want to have thoughts that serve you and help you to achieve career success.

This, then, is Stage 3 in the Career Navigation Model. It can be the toughest stage to deal with, especially if you feel you're working through these issues alone, but we hope our advice below will both inspire and educate you to create possibilities for your future.

I AM HUNGRY FOR A VISION OF WHAT I CAN BE

In Stage 3, you want to remove the limitations you have placed on yourself, and *generate ideas and possibilities* (any ideas: crazy ideas, big ideas, scary ideas, exciting ideas) of what you want to *be* in the short term and longer term. You want to use your understanding of self and of the new world of work to imagine other possibilities for yourself through different combinations of your talents, skills and knowledge. You want to give yourself permission to consider these other possibilities. Through your thoughts, you can start to create a whole new world.

Napoleon Hill once said, 'If your imagination is the mirror of your soul, then you have a perfect right to stand before that mirror and see yourself as you wish to be.'

How you handle this stage will determine whether you will escape The Trap or not. It will determine whether you will have the opportunity to do what you love or not. It will determine whether you will make a contribution.

Your limited vision can trap you and you can remain fearfully in your comfort zone. Or you can adopt the 'I create career success' mindset and commit to creating possibilities.

A word of warning: it does take more energy and effort to think beyond the immediate situation. It is easier to think about your problems than to imagine possible solutions. You can reduce the energy required to picture solutions by using visuals, removing distractions, getting things out of your head and on to paper.

THEATRE OF DREAMS

'As humans we have the power to change our world as we have the ability to imagine better.' So said, J K Rowling in her speech at the 2008 Harvard commencement address. So often, people forget to use this power. They find themselves trapped and unable to move forward.

The more you are able to draw on the vast capacity of your brain, the more you will be able to visualise new possibilities for the short or longer term. You will be able to transcend time and your current situation, imagining a future for yourself. You will be able to synthesise your understanding of yourself and the world of work, seeing connections as you look at the bigger picture.

To help you to unleash this power, we must introduce you to the Theatre of Dreams. The Theatre of Dreams has a big movie screen, big comfy chairs, loads of popcorn and endless viewing time. You need to visit this theatre on a regular basis to allow connections to form and to play with possibilities.

Now it is your turn in the Theatre of Dreams.

Prepare to enter your Theatre of Dreams

Before you can enter your Theatre of Dreams, you need to remove yourself from your day-to-day routine, relax and switch off your logical brain. If you have done a good job of gaining knowledge and understanding in Stages 1 and 2 of the Career Navigation Model, you have what you need to enter the Theatre of Dreams. Take off your work clothes and put on your play clothes. Quieten your mind and get ready to play.

It is all just invented

In the Theatre of Dreams, you can be whatever you want to be. Settle down to watch yourself on the movie screen as you take on many roles and careers. Try on ideas, as a child would try on costumes in a dress-up studio.

Suspend all judgement and don't try to finalise anything. Just play. Anticipate that negative thoughts will be running around in your brain, such as, 'But I could never ...', 'I don't think it is realistic ...', 'I don't think it will be possible ...', 'But I would need to ...', 'My husband will never agree ...', 'I just can't do this now ...'. Remember that this is just a game – there is no need for panic. Have some popcorn.

Play around with how you could use your talents, skills and knowledge in differing roles, companies, industries and work environments. Imagine combining some of your skills with different knowledge. Consider your natural roles and how you could use them in different environments with different goals.

Remember a time you were happy in your work. What were you doing? How can you do that in a different way at this stage in your life?

Think of a scenario you would enjoy. Cross boundaries and make new connections. Play around with changing your goals. Look at the big picture and see what contributions you can make, what needs you could meet and what value could you offer. What would you look like if you were engaged? What would you be doing? Imagine your ideal work day. Play around with different combinations of possibilities.

Be aware of possibilities that leave you feeling curious. Allow them to float into your consciousness. Don't scrutinise them – just notice them. As you play, they should become clearer so that they can be described in words.

Some of what you visualise will make you squirm or laugh out loud or feel scared. Maybe you will need to push the fast-forward button if you can't stand to watch anymore. Does your heart pound? Are you smiling or frowning? Are you making some weird connections?

Replay your favourites

Most people have their favourite movies or shows that they love to watch time and time again. Maybe they love the funny lines or the music or how they feel when they watch a particular scene. Something brings us back to their favourites.

In your Theatre of Dreams, replay the movies of you that you love. Something about that movie makes you want to replay it or relive it. It doesn't matter what draws you back, just watch it again and again. Notice how you are powerfully in action and *alive*. Replay your favourites until you can say in words what you desire – just like ordering a meal from a waiter.

A memory

Like taking a photo of a memorable day, before you leave the Theatre of Dreams, create a spidergram or a model, or download a picture from the Internet that captures how you envisioned yourself while playing out your favourite ideas. Don't rely on your own memory of your best dream – memories are fickle and can lie. We have found that, however weird it feels, this exercise works best when people create a physical memento of their thoughts about future possibilities. These mementos become powerful reminders later, when the moment has passed.

How did it go?

If it was your first time in the Theatre of Dreams, it is likely you found it a struggle. Many people are not used to using their right-brain hemispheres in this way. It may feel unnatural and foggy. You may need some practice. Maybe you lack patience and want a quick-fix solution. You may want to ask yourself what is keeping you from playing with possibilities. Maybe this is blocking your career success. Luckily, you can go back again to play.

As you get better at it, you will notice that you may be curious about what you saw in the Theatre of Dreams and that you want to go back to develop it further. You may not be able to describe it properly yet. You may have seen something amazing that you want to pursue. You may also have had an insight and feel inspired to make it happen.

The how of insights – adapted from *Your Brain At Work* by David Rock (Harper, 2009)

Dr Beeman is one of the world's experts on the neuroscience of insights. Dr Beeman says that an insight experience is characterised by 'a lack of logical progression to the solution but instead a sudden "knowing" regarding the answer'. Everyone knows that feeling of an answer popping into their awareness when they least expect it – like in the shower or on a walk, or even as they're just falling asleep.

Beeman found that people who solved problems with insight had more activation of a brain region called the right anterior temporal lobe. This area allows a person to pull distantly related information together. It is the part of the right-brain hemisphere which is associated with holistic connections.

Career navigators are prone to focus in on the details of the dilemma instead of the big picture. Here, then, are some tips to encourage the formation of connections and insights:

- Reduce your anxiety. Have some fun and take the pressure off yourself by taking a walk, listening to music or baking a cake.
- As much as possible, switch off your logical thought processes and detailed thinking. Stop analysing and thinking about a solution from the past as this may be exactly what is stopping you coming up with a new, more effective strategy. Make space for new thinking.
- Quieten your mind and see what is there in the more subtle connections. Beeman noted that those who are able to observe their thinking, and thus change how they think, are more likely to have insights, as they have better cognitive control, leading to a quieter mind.
- Focus on the connections between information, rather than the problem. Look at the patterns and links from a vantage point, rather than drilling down into the detail.
- Vague ideas, connections and thoughts may start to form. Allow them to come into your consciousness. Allow them to be there without scrutiny. See where they lead you.

Blockages

There are three things that can block your imagination in the Theatre of Dreams: lack of knowledge; fear of what you may find and lack of creativity.

Lack of knowledge

Your brain needs knowledge and understanding to create connections. The more you stimulate the brain, the more you will make connections and see opportunities. If you don't have adequate knowledge and understanding of self and the world of work, you may need to do more work in these areas.

These are some resources that may assist you to gain more knowledge and understanding:

- Review the results of individual career assessments and psychometric tests.
- Review your Self-Q tool or any other self-awareness tool.
- Read about the current and future world of work.
- Research certain careers and what tasks they involve.
- Arrange job shadows and other practical experiences.
- Hold relevant discussions with friends and family.
- Hold relevant discussions at work (with a coach, a mentor, an HR representative, your boss, other managers or colleagues).
- Review organisational charts and standard career paths or job frameworks.
- Review the strategy of the business and, if possible, the strategy of the competitors.
- Watch and learn from role models and inspiring people in your community.
- Identify 'ideas people' in your network and ask them for ideas.
- Network (including ex-colleagues, those a few years ahead of you and university contacts). The more central you are in the network, the more ideas will come your way.
- Read articles and books by industry experts and industry bodies.
- Hold discussions with recruitment companies.
- Watch TED videos for inspiration (www.ted.com).
- Discuss learning and career-enhancing opportunities.
- Remember the dreams you had when you were young. What have you always wanted to be?

Fear of what you may find

Fear is such a dominant force in career navigation and it limits many people's actions and thinking. You now know that, by limiting your thinking, you limit what may be possible for you. Maybe you sat in the Theatre of Dreams and only saw your fears. Maybe your fears are trapping you and possibly even overwhelming you.

We propose an approach, outlined by Rick Carson, in *Taming the Gremlin* (Quill, 2003), which has worked effectively for many fearful career navigators.

He explains how you need to identify your fear, separate it from yourself and then create a visual of it. Maybe it looks like an ugly purple dinosaur or a train roaring towards you. Notice where it is in relation to you and its favourite tunes. Maybe it sings, 'You are not good enough,' or 'You are going to fail.'

Now take control of it. Place it where it will not hinder you. Maybe you need it in the room to motivate you but you don't need it in your head, dominating you. You can lock it away, break it down, ignore it, put it to work for you or, as one career navigator did, shoot it at dawn. Refer to Rick Carson's book for a greater understanding of his technique.

You want to find a way to dominate your fears otherwise they will dominate you.

Rightsizing Your Passion

'Excitement about goals is often diminished by our fear of failure or the drudgery of work. If you're short on passion, it might be because your goals are too small or the fear is too big.

'Do a job for a long time and achieve what you set out to achieve, and suddenly, the dream job becomes a trudge instead. The job hasn't changed – your dreams have.

'Mostly, though, it's about our fear. Fear is the dream killer, the silent voice that pushes us to lose our passion in a vain attempt to seek safety.

'While you can work hard to dream smaller dreams, I think it's better to embrace the fear and find bigger goals instead.'
Seth Godin's Blog, 4 February 2012

Lack of creativity

Clearly, to achieve this goal of creating possibilities, you're going to need some creativity. According to Richard Florida, author of *Rise of the Creative Class* (Basic Books, 2002) more than 50% of today's workers (in developed economies or industries) do creative work. However, with the amount of change in business these days, even the non-creative people increasingly run into brand-new problems; problems with no procedures to follow and no obvious answers. All career navigators are doing creative work as they seek to generate ideas and possibilities for themselves. But how can you do it better?

MORE POSSIBILITIES

Connecting the unconnected

Daniel H Pink, in his book *A Whole New Mind* (Penguin Books, 2006), identifies six essential aptitudes for what he calls 'the Conceptual Age'. One of the aptitudes of right-brained people is 'Symphony', which he defines as 'the ability to put the pieces together. It is the capacity to synthesise rather than analyse; to see relationships between seemingly unrelated fields; to detect broad patterns rather than deliver specific answers, and to invent something new by combining elements nobody else thought to pair.'

Mihalyi Csikszentmihalyi studied the lives of creative people and, in his book *Flow: The Psychology of Optimal Experience* (HarperCollins, 2008), notes that 'creativity generally involves crossing the boundaries of domains'. Creative people are also able to see relationships that others don't notice and are able to link seemingly unconnected ideas to create new concepts and opportunities. Boundary-crossers, according to Pink, 'reject either/or choices and seek multiple options and blended solutions'.

When career navigators cross boundaries, they blend their talents, skills and knowledge together to create a unique offering. Career navigators seek to develop the ability to synthesise and link apparently unconnected elements to generate more possibilities.

Suggestions to achieve this are:

* Extract your talents from the Self-Q tool and put the keywords down one half of a piece of paper. On the other half, list your knowledge. Identify five different ways you could combine your talents and knowledge to play different roles. For example, you may be working in an IT company, using your talent of relating to others and building relationships to provide customer services. You could use your knowledge of the company products and customer needs in combination with your strategic talent to allow you to identify various

alternatives for moving forward and joining the product development team.

- Explore the intersection of your talents. What key aspects from your Self-Q tool could you combine to create a competitive advantage or to fill a gap in the market? How could you combine aspects of yourself to be unique?

- Get a newspaper or printout from the jobs website (such as www.careerjunction.co.za) and make a list of job openings that interest you. Would these jobs require your talents? Could you upskill or reskill to be able to do any of these jobs?

- Extract your interests and the challenges that interest you from your Self-Q tool. Compare this to your list of your talents. How could you use your talents and abilities to work in your areas of interest? What are the possible jobs, hobbies or activities that a person with those interests could pursue? What additional skills and knowledge would you need to develop? For example, you may be interested in process efficiencies. You could use your ability to create new processes as a full-time employee. You could research more efficient processes and publish your research. You could contract to a company and use your analytical and communication talents to scrutinise current processes and provide a report on their current process efficiency. You could project manage the implementation of new processes.

- Extract your natural roles from the Self-Q tool and identify jobs in the new world of work which would allow you to play your natural role.

- Review the roles and activities that you really enjoyed in previous jobs. What activities were you doing that you really enjoyed? In what other companies or industries could you do these same activities?

SOUTH AFRICAN EXAMPLES

Dr Michael Mol is a well-known South African TV presenter, best known for anchoring *Top Billing*, the longest-running lifestyle show in South Africa's history. He is also a personal friend of Graeme, having known each other since they were kids. Michael's remarkable life story is of someone who has had the foresight, and guts, to follow his career aspirations and look for the career 'symphony' that Daniel Pink talks about.

Michael left school wanting to become a medical doctor and worked at that dream with characteristic enthusiasm and dedication. Having qualified, he pursued a specialty in trauma medicine, showing an interest in adrenalin-inducing activities and high-stress situations. As a dare from some friends, he entered the Mr South Africa competition, and, to his surprise, actually won the competition. This gave him a year in the limelight and a taste of a different type of adrenalin and stress in front of the camera. He was then offered the anchor role at *Top Billing* and decided to make the career shift to media.

But Michael wanted to ensure that his career in medicine continued. Like many people, he found himself conflicted between competing career options. He spent some time working in a business consultancy and was soon snapped up by one of their clients, an international wellness and nutrition company, where he was appointed as MD. So he had three sets of career tools: medicine, media and business skills.

His latest career choice is a wonderful example of pulling all the threads of a career path together. In 2011, Michael returned to the media to host a show called *Hello Doctor*. This is a TV show that aims to provide vital medical information on important health issues, and features celebrities raising the profile of diseases and medical issues they've faced. It pushes all of Michael's buttons, plays to all his strengths and is a wonderful example of someone who refused to stop searching for a career that made the most of all he wanted to be.

Gary Bailey is the best goalkeeper South African football has ever produced. His greatest ambition growing up was to be a professional footballer, although he also enjoyed studying. After school, he studied at university during the day and played part-time professional football in the evenings. That lifestyle changed dramatically when he signed for Manchester United. Gary has commented many times that his 10 years there were the ultimate in terms of football experience, but did nothing to further his desire to be mentally stimulated and stretched. And so he was keen to retire and enter into a more 'thinking' type of environment.

He started a company, teaching business skills to low-level miners, but this job left out his real passion for football. So after 18 months, he passed on the business to his partner and proceeded to look for a job in the radio/TV broadcasting field – something that would involve sport and being mentally active. It was a financial gamble, and involved starting off on the lowest rung in a radio news room (not easy at 30 and after having been a top soccer star), but he gradually got the hang of it. After four years, he progressed to a top presenter job, covering football on TV. Gary explains, 'This I have enjoyed doing for the last 20 years, and more recently I have added motivational speaking to companies, using soccer and my time with Sir Alex Ferguson to create a second income stream. Again I have mixed being mentally stimulated with my passion for football, and have also made myself less susceptible to the vulnerabilities of the TV public.'

As you create your own dream career, take inspiration from both Michael and Gary, and don't stop seeking a career that makes the best use of *all* the skills, dreams and aspirations you have.

LOOKING AT THE BIGGER PICTURE

If you only think about how you could use your talents for your own benefit, you will only ever identify a subset of possibilities. You should expand your view further and consider how you can use your talents and efforts in service of something greater than yourself.

We're sure you've heard the story of the three stonecutters. One day, a traveller was walking along a lane and came across three stonecutters working in a quarry. Each was busy cutting a block of stone. Interested to find out what they were working on, he asked the first stonecutter what he was doing.

'I am cutting a stone!' Still no wiser the traveller turned to the second stonecutter and asked him what he was doing.

'I am cutting this block of stone to make sure that it is square, and its dimensions are uniform, so that it will fit exactly in its place in a wall.'

A bit closer to finding out what the stonecutters were working on but still unclear, the traveller turned to the third stonecutter. He seemed to be the happiest of the three and when asked what he was doing replied, 'I am building a cathedral.'

It's an old story, but it perfectly illustrates what you should be aiming for. Creating possibilities isn't just about coming up with a list of things you could do. It's about finding the few things that will be the best things for you to do.

Our experience is that this is most likely to happen when the career you envisage and pursue is one that is not only fulfilling for you, but also makes a contribution. This is when true meaning and purpose seem to emerge.

Until recently, many career navigators would not have given thought to the contribution that they make – or wish to make – to the whole (their community, society, country or planet). Having a purpose or finding meaning in work would have been considered an optional extra. A nice to have. Relevant to the lucky few. This is no longer the case, as finding meaning in work has become a key component of any career decision. Let's understand why this is.

Company perspective

Management is slowly evolving from focusing on employee competence (ability to do work) to employee commitment (willingness to do work). Companies are noticing that, if people perceive their work to have meaning or enjoy their work, they are more dedicated, fulfilled and engaged in their work. Meaning, therefore, has market value as it increases engagement and productivity, thereby increasing customer satisfaction and shareholder wealth. As companies start to understand this link, they will want to employ people who find meaning or enjoyment in their work.

Dave Ulrich and Wendy Ulrich said in their book, *The Why of Work* (McGraw-Hill, 2010), 'Meaning has *market value*. Meaningful work solves real problems, contributes real benefits and thus adds real value to customers and investors. Employees who find meaning in their work are more satisfied, more engaged, and in turn more productive. They work smarter, harder, more passionately and creatively. They learn and adapt. They are more connected to customer needs. And they stick around.'

Meaning-making is becoming a priority for companies as it impacts their bottom-line profits.

Individual perspective

As people face the increased demands of the world of work, including increased working hours, they need the additional energy and commitment that comes from finding meaning in their work. Feelings of frustration, depression and emptiness come from a lack of a clear line of sight between their efforts and what matters most to them. More people are seeking – and, in increasing numbers, demanding – a clear line of sight between what they do and what they value, or what outcomes matter most to them.

Some people find meaning and motivation by using their talents in the workplace. Others, as Daniel H Pink suggests in his book *Drive*, find motivation in having autonomy or an opportunity to master skills or talents. Other career navigators are looking for a purpose greater than themselves. Dr Martin Seligman, the father of positive psychology says, 'The pleasant life: a life that successfully pursues the positive emotions about the present, past, and future. The good life: using your signature strengths to obtain abundant gratification in the main realms of your life. The meaningful life: using your signature strengths and virtues in the service of something much larger than you are.'

We have noticed that career navigators who are powerfully in action are most likely to be those who are using their strengths in service of something greater than themselves. There are many different ways in which this can be done.

As you review our ideas on serving the whole, remember Viktor Frankl's words: 'Ask not what is the meaning of life but rather what is my meaning to life.' The next time you enter the Theatre of Dreams you may want to play with possibilities for serving the whole.

Meet a need

Work for a company or organisation whose services or products meet a need that you believe to be important. Examples include providing fresh and healthy food, caring for the sick, teaching and developing skills, or protection services such as physical and asset protection.

Contribute to a better life

Work for a company or organisation whose services contribute to a better life for others. This may include developing infrastructure or a drug to cure a disease; raising awareness of important issues; developing banking products or skills development programmes that allow the poor to improve their standard of living, or improving access to water, healthcare and safety through IT or telecommunications.

For example, Mohammed Yunus, a Bangladeshi economist, founded the Grameen Bank which provides small loans to poor people lacking collateral, in an effort to enable them to establish their creditworthiness and become financially self-sufficient. This company has positively contributed to improve the lives of the poor and for this Yunus and the bank won the Nobel Peace Prize in 2006.

Alignment

Work for a company that pursues what is being called 'the triple bottom line'. This is where three distinct purposes are given equal priority: profits, people and the planet.

For example, Nedbank wants to become a leader in sustainability. They seek to impact people, the environment, economics and the country positively. They have become known as the green bank and are intent on making a green impact. View their sustainability journey on their website www.nedbankgroup.co.za.

By choosing a company such as this as your employer (or even by choosing them as your bank), you are supporting their initiatives and you, too, are becoming a contributor towards sustainability.

Social responsibility programmes

Work for a company that supports social responsibility programmes, either through profit contributions, company resources or their employee's time.

For example, Internet Solutions provides IT support and company resources called Infinite Family (www.infinitefamily.org), assisting with a mentoring programme for disadvantaged youth. Infinite Family recently won a CNN Hero Award.

PricewaterhouseCoopers' survey of 4 271 graduates entitled 'Managing Tomorrow's People: Millennials at Work' (see www.pwc.com/managingpeople 2020) reports that 86% of new college hires will seek employers with social responsibility values that reflect their own, and will consider leaving an employer whose social responsibility values no longer reflect their own.

Most companies are expanding their social responsibility programmes by embedding leadership development opportunities into these programmes.

Start your own company

By creating your own company and creating jobs, you can uplift families and communities.

Yashwin Mohan, entrepreneur at the Branson Centre of Entrepreneurship and founder of Game Over says in Richard Branson's *Screw Business as Usual* (Random House, 2011), 'The Branson Centre has contributed to my success. I can now create jobs for people that I've hired and the impact this has on their lives and the lives of their families and their communities is enormous.'

Social entrepreneur

Become a social entrepreneur. This is a person (or organisation) who, as defined by Wikipedia, 'recognises a social problem and uses entrepreneurial and business principles to organise, create and manage a venture to achieve social change and solve a societal problem. While a business entrepreneur typically measures performance in profit and return, a social entrepreneur focuses on creating social capital'.

For example, Brent Freeman, Norma LaRosa, and Nick Reder are the co-founders of Roozt.com, an e-commerce site that allows online shoppers to buy from socially responsible entrepreneurs and donate to a monthly cause. Every day shoppers can now make a difference with their shopping expenditure.

Personal commitment

Commit to a set of beliefs or principles. Commit to overcoming a challenge that we face in society, raising awareness or exposing the truth.

For example, Andrew Sykes runs a USA-based company called Health at Work (www.healthatwork.com), which aims to make people more aware of their health and as a result more healthy. The company designs and implements programmes in the workplace to encourage healthier living. Andrew, an actuary and professional speaker, is an example of a person who is committed to a belief that health matters, and uses this belief and his keen actuarial mind to find practical solutions to the healthcare crisis being experienced worldwide. Other beliefs and principles may include fairness, simplifying things, improving efficiencies, making others laugh, stretching others to be more, and protecting the innocent.

Remember Nicole from Chapter 1, the 35-year-old divorced lady who wanted to find a job that she enjoyed and which also had good financial prospects.

Nicole asked, 'Are you saying I need to give up my work and start working for a charity?' For some, serving the whole may mean this, but for many people, it requires them to place equal emphasis on purpose and financial rewards. Nicole asked the next logical question, 'What could I do that would pay my bills and allow me to have a purpose?'

In her Theatre of Dreams, she made a connection between doing what she loved and what she valued. She made a connection between protecting the monies of vulnerable people and using her analytical talent. She could see how she could make money and serve the whole in a way she considered to be critical. This connection expanded her thinking on her possibilities. Initially, Nicole looked to create an opportunity for herself in an insurance company or bank, working in forensics or auditing. She found an opportunity in the Office of the Ombud for Financial Services Providers. The FAIS Ombud's role is to resolve disputes between financial services providers and their clients. At the time of publishing this book, she said she is more engaged than ever before as she can see how her efforts protect the monies of vulnerable individuals. She said she is striving to find new ways to provide an improved service.

In the words of US President Woodrow Wilson, 'You are not here merely to make a living. You are here to enable the world to live more amply, with greater vision, and with a finer spirit of hope and achievement. You are here to enrich the world. You impoverish yourself if you forget this errand.'

WHAT THIS MEANS FOR YOU

You can expand your thinking and thereby expand what is possible for you in your career. As the experts have shown, there are ways to improve your creative thought and you can enter the Theatre of Dreams to play with possibilities for the short and longer term. You can make new connections that can change your whole world.

As Viktor Frankl taught, the good news is that the meaning of your life is not controlled by what happens. You can find meaning, purpose and happiness. The bad news is that you have to work at this meaning-making process. No one can do the hard work for you.

Our challenge to you is to expand your thinking and make new connections that will allow you to be engaged in the workplace and serve a purpose greater than yourself.

Thoughts are Things

I hold it true that thoughts are things;
They're endowed with bodies and breath and wings:
And that we send them forth to fill
The world with good results, or ill.
That which we call our secret thought
Speeds forth to earth's remotest spot,
Leaving its blessing or its woes
Like tracks behind it as it goes

We build our future, thought by thought,
For good or ill, yet know it not.
Yet so the universe was wrought
Thought it another name for fate;
Choose then thy destiny and wait,
For love brings love and hate bring hate

Henry van Dyke

COACHES' CORNER
Seeing possibilities

After completing your Self-Q tool and understanding how the new world of work affects you, enter the Theatre of Dreams and imagine yourself in a variety of roles and what may be possible for you.

If you are struggling, sit with it for a while and notice what is preventing you from seeing possibility for yourself. Lack of knowledge? Fear? Lack of creativity?

Once you have identified these, go back to that section in this chapter and do some of the exercises to overcome this blockage.

Searching for meaning

How can you create meaning in your life by finding a direct link between what you value and what you do each day? Start by making a list of 5 to 10 things that you value, support or enjoy discussing.

Now that you know what you value, start to find ways to link your daily effort to this value.

Expanding thinking

These words are taken from *The Art of Possibility* by Rosamund Stone Zander and Benjamin Zander (Penguin Books, 2000):

Ask yourself this question

What assumption am I making,
that I am not aware I'm making
That gives me what I see?

And then ask

What might I now invent
That I haven't invented
That would give me other choices?

Being a contribution

Decide to be a contribution in your work in the week ahead. What would that mean you would do differently?

MAIN POINTS

You can expand your thinking and thereby expand what is possible for you in your career.

You can create more possibilities by increasing your knowledge, managing your fear and becoming more creative through connecting the previously unconnected.

More is possible if you consider the bigger picture. The search for meaning is no longer only a matter for the individual only but, as it contributes positively to market value, it now also becomes of importance to companies.

The key to achieving career success and fulfilment is to direct your thoughts to change the outcomes and your feelings about those outcomes. You want to take on the director's role in your brain and no longer be the slave to your limiting stories or negative thoughts. You want to have thoughts that serve you and help you to achieve career success.

SUGGESTED READING

Screw Business as Usual by Richard Branson (Random House, 2011)
Loving What Is by Byron Katie (Rider, 2002)
Man's Search for Meaning by Viktor Frankl (Rider, 2008)
A Whole New Mind by Daniel H Pink (Penguin Books, 2006)
The Why of Work by Dave Ulrich and Wendy Ulrich (McGraw-Hill, 2010)
Your Brain at Work by David Rock (HarperCollins, 2009)
Learned Optimism by Martin E P Seligman (Vintage, 2006)
A New Earth: Awakening to Your Life Purpose by Eckhart Tolle (Penguin Books, 2005)
One Person/Multiple Careers: A New Model for Work/Life Success by Marci Alboher (Warner Business Books, 2007)

A BIT OF INSPIRATION

'Opportunity is missed by most people because it is dressed in overalls and looks like work.' *Thomas A Edison*

6

STAGE 4: MAKING IT HAPPEN

'Somehow I can't believe that there are any heights that can't be scaled by a
man who knows the secrets of making dreams come true.'
Walt Disney

'Success in business requires training and discipline
and hard work. But if you're not frightened by these things,
the opportunities are just as great today as they ever were.'
David Rockefeller

'The harder I practise, the luckier I get.'
Gary Player

'I posted my résumé online and sent it to two different companies and I have not heard anything. I am so frustrated and depressed. Do you think there is something wrong with me? Do you think I should try another career portal? I hear there is a better one that just started.'

Many career navigators take limited action to make their ideas a reality. If you really want to achieve career success as defined by you, you will actively need to make it happen. Posting a résumé on a career portal is not sufficient, and is the fastest route to killing your self-esteem. You need more strategies and you need more action.

Stage 4 of the Career Navigation Model is 'Making it Happen', and requires you to clarify your ideas, investigate what is needed to turn the ideas into reality, and then take steps over a short or longer term to secure work that will allow you to be engaged. Some ideas can be developed in the short term and others will take time to brew to perfection slowly.

Successful career navigators may start with a vague idea of what they want to *be* and they then move deliberately and strategically towards implementing their ideas. By developing their ideas, learning about the world of work, building self-awareness, networking, and gaining skills and knowledge, they crystallise their ideas. And then, through sufficient, appropriate action and follow-through, their ideas become a reality.

INSTANT GRATIFICATION

Beware of The Trap: you may have an idea, but when opportunities don't *immediately* materialise, you may get sidetracked, forget about your idea or lose focus, find a quicker and easier job option, and tumble backwards into The Trap.

We live in an age of instant gratification. We want everything instantly and without effort, and we bristle when others around us appear to be getting more, sooner. Waiting for rewards or results is frustrating. But this 'instant' mentality is very detrimental to the majority of career navigators. Most career success comes from hundreds of consistent small efforts that eventually grow into a series of satisfying wins.

Very few people get to escape the effort required to become a success. Instead of looking for shortcuts to success, you need to manage your success actively.

MAKING IT HAPPEN

In Stage 3, you entered the Theatre of Dreams and created connections and possibilities. Before you can powerfully choose any of these possibilities, you need to clarify your ideas and gain understanding about what it will take to make these ideas into a reality. You may need to take a few steps to gain more understanding and certainty. You may also need to target specific development opportunities to make certain opportunities more accessible. You may, at this stage, still have a number of possibilities and that is acceptable.

DEFINITE AIM

In Lewis Carroll's famous book, *Alice in Wonderland*, the heroine finds herself lost. Alice approaches the grinning Cheshire cat to ask directions. When the cat asks where she is trying to go, Alice isn't quite sure. The cat provocatively states the obvious: it doesn't matter which road Alice takes if she doesn't know where she wants to end up. Some career navigators struggle with the idea of having, committing to, or believing in achieving a definite aim. They say they will just go with the flow.

You can still achieve career success without a definite aim. However, those who know *what* they want and *who* they want to *be* seem to gain momentum through their focus, have more persistence and, as a result, more success. As Napoleon Hill said in his book *The Law of Success* (first published in 1928, with many updates):

> If success depends upon power and if power is organised effort and if the
> first step in the direction of organisation is a definite purpose then one may
> easily see why such a purpose is essential ... There is a psychological, as
> well as an economic, reason for the selection of a definite aim in life. It is a
> well-established principle of psychology that a person's acts are always in
> harmony with the dominating thoughts of his mind. Any definite chief aim
> that is deliberately fixed in the mind, and held there with the determination to
> realise it, finally saturates the entire subconscious mind until it automatically
> influences the physical action of the body towards the attainment of that
> purpose.

A definite aim is a vivid, idealised description of a desired outcome. It should inspire, energise and help you to create a mental picture of your target. For most career navigators, a mental or printed picture is the most effective way of encapsulating their desires or definite aims. The image may be shaking hands on a business deal, buying a holiday home or receiving an award or affirmation.

You want to be as specific as possible with your mental image of your definite aim. If you seek money, then identify exactly how much money you desire. If you seek affirmation, then identify for what and by whom. If you want to change the world, then be specific about the type of change you want to see. If you seek a certain role, then identify the skills you will possess, what you will be doing and how others will be responding. Notice how you will feel and where you will be. The point is to be specific.

Some people vaguely define their aim as financial security. This is vague and wishful. You need to be very specific in your definite aim by answering questions such as 'How much money do I require to be financially secure?', 'By when?', 'What am I going to do to get the money?', 'What need will I be meeting?'. Return to your Theatre of Dreams and create a clear, definite aim.

CLARITY

Tommy Franks said, 'Courage has to do with controlling fear and it seems to me that focus has a way of overcoming anxiety.'

As the clarity of your definite aim increases, your anxiety, restlessness and stress levels will decrease. If you don't believe us, try it for yourself. It works for us, and for hundreds of people we've worked with. We are not suggesting that clarity will allow you to be relaxing with a glass of your favourite beverage for longer periods, but rather that you will be very busy making it happen with less anxiety, deep-seated stress or disease. What if all your health problems were a result of your lack of a definite aim? Maybe achieving clarity on your definite aim is worth a try. The Theatre of Dreams awaits you.

Tanya, introduced in Chapter 1, was a frustrated nurse seeking direction for her future. She completed the Self-Q tool and entered the Theatre of Dreams. She played with the idea of developing her management skills and running the hospital. She played with the idea of doing art and providing art lessons. She played with making a connection between her two great loves: caring for others and art. An idea of combining post-operative care and art using art therapy arose. Based on her idea, Tanya needed to create and write down her definite aim. This involved creating a vivid, idealised description of a desired outcome that inspired, energised and helped her to create a mental picture. After further thought she captured her definite aim as earning US$5 000 per month after taxes while providing art therapy to patients in *her* post-operative care facility. She put a five-year timeframe on this. She found an image that portrayed her definite aim and she placed it near her dresser.

It's so easy to do what's familiar, comfortable or fun. It's so difficult, sometimes, to tackle the highest priority and work towards your definite aim. You may be tempted by a comfortable or more secure job. You may be struggling to move towards your definite aim and be lost in the problems.

You need to decide upon steps or actions that you are going to take to get to your definite aim and be ready to make choices and accept opportunities.

Information gathering

For a person seeking to secure a role, this may entail gathering information about the skills; knowledge and experience required; the relevant courses available; the contacts who can assist to secure this role, as well as the financial package. These days, prospective employers expect you to have done quite a lot of homework on any job you might be applying for, so if you're aiming to work in a specific industry or company, research about that role is essential.

For a person thinking of starting a new business, or being a self-employed contractor, this may include gathering information about the products and services currently being offered (your competitors and the marketplace); the industry prospects; financial and product information to complete a business plan, and the requirements for starting a business.

See www.mindofafox.com (especially the Conversation Model) for a suggested 10-step process for doing this, courtesy of Clem Sunter. To get a model business plan format, you can look at the resources available from www.inc.com (a magazine aimed at small businesses), especially www.inc.com/tools/business-model-template.html or the resources available at www.entrepreneurmag.co.za. If you have an iPad and are prepared to spend a little bit more money (currently US$30 at time of writing) for a top-class digital system, then consider using Business Model Toolbox (www.businessmodelgeneration.com).

Gap analysis

Determine the gap: the difference between where you are and where you want to be (your definite aim). Identify what you need to acquire in terms of skills, knowledge, experience, contacts and ideas. Then set about creating a high-level plan for how you intend to close the gap and reach your definite aim.

Experiment

If you are considering changing your career or role, you may want to create an 'experimental phase' when you get to try different options out for a brief time.

Companies use a similar concept with a new idea and refer to it as an incubator phase. During this time, you may work on your idea in addition to your normal workload: job shadow, do voluntary work or probation work, or offer to work on a related project in your company. Give yourself an opportunity to experience, for a short time, a particular role that interests you. If you realise fairly quickly that it's not for you, then get out of the experiment as soon as possible and cross it off your list of possibilities.

GETTING A FOOT IN THE DOOR

It is likely you will need strategies to get your foot in the door at a potential employer or client. You are seeking to attract the attention of those with the power to hire you as well as other influential players in the industry. In all your efforts to attract attention, focus on how *you* can solve the problems the company is facing, meet their need for skills and ideas, or be of value in any other way.

Prepare a good 'elevator speech'

If you found yourself in an elevator with someone significant (the CEO of a company you're trying to work for, for example), and he or she asked you, 'So, what do you do?' and then pressed the button for the eighth floor, what would you say before the elevator stopped? That's your 'elevator speech'. It's about 30 seconds long and gets the other person intrigued enough to say, 'I'd love to hear more.' It doesn't tell them everything about you; it is designed only to get them to remember you and be interested in spending more time with you. Have a look at the steps outlined by Harvard Business School for creating an elevator speech and give it a go on www.alumni.hbs.edu/careers/pitch.

Create an interesting résumé and clever video

You need to create an interesting résumé or clever video to create an impression with potential employers and grab their attention.

Have a look at these two examples of interesting résumés:

- www.businessinsider.com/insanely-creative-resumes-2011-6#eric-gandhi-landed-an-interview-at-google-with-this-one-4 (also look forward

and backwards in this slide show for other examples).
* www.youtube.com/watch?v=9EzNll1U2N8.

If you are struggling with the design of your résumé, there are companies that will assist you to design a more interesting one. Have a look at www.elance.com or www.behance.net for a freelance designer to give your résumé a makeover.

Note that the style of your résumé should match the company, industry and role that you are applying for. Many of the examples of very creative formats were made by creative people applying for creative jobs. This might not be as applicable for accountants, lawyers or dentists.

Network

Your strategy should include making use of networks (online or face-to-face). This can open up amazing opportunities for the career navigator, particularly at this stage. Networking can assist in gathering information and making contacts who can help you to achieve your definite aim. Through networking, you want to attract the attention of or make contact with the person who has the power to hire you.

There are many real-world networking opportunities that you can take advantage of, including small business networks, meeting people from your profession, chambers of commerce in your local area, or conferences on particular topics of interest to you. Some of these cost a bit of money but many are free. You should aim to attend some of these and ensure you have a pile of business cards to hand out.

At this stage of your career navigation, your personal business contact card should have your contact details on the one side, and on the back, a bulleted list of your capabilities and career aspirations (similar to your elevator speech). Be memorable.

In this digital age, there are also other ways to network that are not quite as draining as networking events are for most people. Companies are attracting, sourcing and recruiting candidates through social networks such as Facebook, LinkedIn and Second Life. As you navigate your career, you want to use these networks to create a professional online presence. You want to take part in the online conversation to create quality contacts and to show your expertise.

Being active in online groups improves your profile and is especially effective if future employers are also in the group.

It also opens you up to what researchers call 'weak links'. These are vitally important links in real-world networks, such as people you went to school with or family friends. In their book *Connected* (Little Brown and Company, 2009), Christakis and Fowler show the surprising power of these real-world social networks and how they shape our lives:

> Weaker connections frequently act as bridges from one group to another and therefore play a critical role. [In a survey of] several technical, managerial and professional workers who had recently relied on a personal contact to get a new job [they] asked them a simple question: 'Prior to switching employers, how often did you see the person who helped you get the new job?' [They] found that only 17% responded 'often', while 55% responded 'occasionally' and the remaining 28% said 'rarely'. Most workers found jobs via old college friends, past workmates or previous employers ... It is remarkable that people receive crucial information from individuals whose very existence they have forgotten.

Online social networking has allowed many of us to develop quite extensive and powerful weak links within our networks. We believe that it is essential to create, manage and constantly maintain your online social networks if you want work in the 21st century. This is not a book about how to manage your online social media presence, or an introduction to these tools if you don't use them yet, but here are a few tips that might assist you:

Tips for online social media presence

- Keep your profiles clean. If you're going to want potential employers to have a look at your profile, then make sure they'll like what they see. That doesn't mean you can't comment on that party or upload a crazy photo – but just make sure you'd be happy with someone who has the power to hire you knowing that part of who you are.
- Make your profile interesting. Employers will be looking for a candidate who is social and outgoing; someone with character, who stands out from the crowd.

- Spread yourself around. Use Facebook and LinkedIn, obviously. But also consider Google+, Twitter, About.me, YouTube and consider setting up a blog as well.
- Check what someone will see when they google your name. Work hard to get more information and profile data onto the web.
- Connect with the companies you're interested in. Like their Facebook pages, follow their Twitter streams and join their LinkedIn groups.

Tips for using Facebook to open doors and job possibilities

- You want to extend your friends to include friends of friends and the weak ties identified in the research above.
- Complete the 'About me' sections fully (including your elevator pitch) and don't be scared to let the world know your definite aim.
- Once you have built your network of friends, you can make use of applications on Facebook like BranchOut and BeKnown to show you who may be useful contacts in your network.
- Ask people to help you.

Tips for using LinkedIn to navigate your career

- There are tools on LinkedIn that will show a recruiter that you are in the job market. See www.linkedin.com/jobs.
- Join an open group on LinkedIn for your industry or preferred career. Follow influential players in this industry and join the conversation. Collaborate to solve real issues and real problems. In other words, join groups and make contributions (ask and answer questions, and interact with the other group members).
- Start following the HR manager, hiring manager or team leaders in the companies you wish to work for. They are generally more accepting of online communication via LinkedIn as it is a business network.

Use career or job portals

Consider joining a career or job portal, such as CareerJunction, Careers24 and Pnet. These are websites where employers can post job offers, and people looking for employment can post their skills.

Three tips for using career portals

- Have a keyword-rich résumé. For example, if you are a sales rep, make sure you have 'account executive', 'business development', 'new business' and 'account manager' on your résumé.
- Update regularly. Portals have a very limited search engine so make sure you update your résumé on regular basis as recruiters may only look for résumés updated in the last three to six months. At the very least, you should change and add keywords once a quarter to keep it updated.
- Make use of job alerts. When a recruiter loads a job that you may be interested in, then an email is sent to alert you. You can be specific when setting up these alerts by specifying salary, location, and other criteria.

Look at company job boards

Identify companies that you would like to work for and view their online job boards. Set up a Google Alert (www.google.com/alerts) and receive updates on their new jobs and stay informed about their vacancies.

Have an action plan

Lutendo, who we met in Chapter 1, brainstormed with a friend in the graphic design industry on possible ways of securing work. His definite aim was to be employed doing design work within three months. He created and followed this strategy:

- Place résumé on three career portals with keywords such as 'graphic design', 'designer', 'website designer', 'images'.
- Sign up for job alerts for all graphic design positions.
- Research internships for graphic designers online.
- Use Google Alerts to set up the following search: 'internship site: www. ogilvy.co.za'. Identify a further five suitable employers and use Google Alerts to keep up-to-date on their vacancies.
- Join Facebook and become friends with all university contacts. Find out where they are working and how they got their jobs. Ask them to inform me of any job opportunities. Follow up every week.
- Join an open group on LinkedIn for graphic designers. Identify companies I would like to join and, through LinkedIn, find the details of

HR managers and internship managers at identified companies.

- Search online for web designers and review websites for job opportunities
- Call 10 web design companies to see if they have available positions. Submit résumé and follow up.
- Volunteer to do a project so that the company has a chance to assess me. Do an excellent job and be on time!
- Go to the careers support centre at university and ask them for assistance.
- Search online for the industry design body and review their job opportunities and internship opportunities.
- Obtain weekly job adverts from the newspaper.

What is your action plan? There is a lot of work to do in the 'pre-choice' phase. We always remind people, though, of the words of Thomas Edison, 'Opportunity is missed by most people because it is dressed in overalls and looks like work.'

CHOOSING POWERFULLY

Sigmund Freud said, 'When making a decision of minor importance, I have always found it advantageous to consider all the pros and cons. In vital matters, however, such as choice of a mate or a profession, the decision should come from the unconscious, from somewhere within ourselves. In the important decisions of personal life, we should be governed, I think, by the deep inner needs of our nature.'

Some career navigators are presented with opportunity and willingly make the choice, through a leap of considered faith, to commit themselves to making their visions realities. Sadly, other career navigators never make a choice and, in this state of indecision, waste resources and years of their lives.

If you've done all the work we've suggested in the first three stages of the Career Navigation Model, and especially if you know you've worked hard at the pre-choice stage we've just outlined, then you need to be ready to choose powerfully when options present themselves. If all the hard work is done, this step can be quite easy. If you trust your hard work and go with your gut, you'll probably be right.

Malcom Gladwell wrote a book about this called *Blink* (Penguin Books, 2006). It's about how decisions can be made in just a few seconds. He suggests that when you meet someone for the first time, or walk into a house you are thinking of buying, or read the first few sentences of a book, or consider a career opportunity, or any number of other everyday situations where a decision needs to be made, you actually take just a few seconds to jump to a series of conclusions. Gladwell believes that 'those instant conclusions that we reach are really powerful and really important and, occasionally, really good'.

We have noticed that, when career navigators are calm and prepared to accept themselves, they somehow already know what they truly want to become and, as Sigmund Freud has noted, their choices come from somewhere within themselves. This is the essence of choosing powerfully. This clarity, however, often gets clouded by fear, greed, ego and many other ills that drive career navigators in modern times.

Difference between making a decision and choosing powerfully

There is a difference between making a decision and committing to a choice. When you make a decision, you weigh up the pros and cons. You make a list of both and then, somehow, decide that the pros outweigh the cons. Or, if you're deciding between two options, you compare the lists for both options and see which one wins. Based on this analysis, you make a decision. That's healthy, but the problem is that you don't always put those lists away when you should. This means that new information could tip the scales on the pros versus cons and you should change your decision. It's the 'grass became greener on the other side' phenomenon. Weighing options is smart of course, but at some point we need to choose to stick with our decision, even if the pros and cons change.

When you *choose powerfully*, you close the pros and cons spreadsheet after making a choice and you commit fully to that choice and its consequences. You close off the other options in your mind and, even if new information arrives, you stick with your choice. At first, this may not sound as if it makes sense, but let's turn to research in behavioural psychology to understand why it does.

In his book, *The Paradox of Choice* (HarperCollins, 2005), Barry Schwartz describes how too much choice is leading to lower levels of satisfaction. Here is a story to illustrate the point. A man goes into a store and asks the salesman if they have any blue shirts. 'Do we ever,' the salesman replies and returns with 10 shirts. Dark blue, light blue, blue with white stripes, thin stripes or fat stripes, a checked blue-and-white shirt, a baby-blue shirt and so on. After 10 minutes, the man can't make up his mind and leaves the store.

At the next store, he asks the next salesman the same question. This time the salesman says, 'Yes sir, we have one perfect blue shirt. I'll bring it you to have a look.' The man looks at the shirt, likes it and buys it. It turns out that same design was at the previous store too, but the overwhelming number of choices left the man feeling more regret about all the shirts he was *not* choosing rather than pleasure about the shirt he was about to buy. (See an excellent TED video of Barry Schwartz telling a similar story at www.ted.com/talks/lang/en/barry_schwartz_on_the_paradox_of_choice.html.

It's often the same way with career decisions and choices. If, at some point, you don't decide to stick with a decision and turn it into a choice, you will end up constantly looking at all the possible options that you didn't select and it is often the reason for feeling (unnecessarily) unhappy with your current situation.

If you don't do this, you'll never be fully committed, since you'll always have one eye open for something better that might come along. Waiting for something better to emerge is the best way to avoid making the most of what you have. When it comes to your career, when you do finally find your passion, choose it powerfully and don't look back. There will always be days when it will be easy to imagine how much better the other options that you didn't choose might have turned out. The successful people channel those thoughts into making sure that what they've chosen *is* the best choice, and not lamenting that it might not be so. For many people who come to see us, what we discover is that they've never really made a powerful choice in their lives, and their trap is that they're constantly in the decision-making mode.

SEEKING CAREER-ENHANCING OPPORTUNITIES

Ideally, young adults are looking for jobs or opportunities that will open their eyes to what is possible and, more importantly, what is possible for *them*. Nick Binedell from the Gordon Institute of Business Science speaks of a 'room with a view' to describe a job or opportunity that opens your eyes to the opportunities that exist and what could be possible for you in your career. A 'room with a view' may be provided by a manager, a mentor, a role model, a colleague, a career-development programme such as a Deloitte Graduate Academy, a career-enhancing opportunity such as a cross-functional project or a cross-border project, the opportunity to join multi-layer key talent programmes, or other learning programmes with outcomes.

Both authors of this book have had the opportunity of a 'room with a view' that significantly expanded our vision of what is possible for ourselves and for you. Kerry's opportunity came when she was 26 years old. She joined a team of actuaries as they started a healthcare and actuarial consultancy. She was part of the team as the company expanded into the largest employee benefit consultancy in South Africa and grew significantly offshore in Singapore, Australia and the UK. She managed teams of people and consulted to multinational clients, guided by more experienced consultants and managers. This opportunity helped her to see things differently; helped her to see what is possible and helped her to understand what she needed to be engaged.

Graeme's 'room with a view' came from work he did with futurist, Wolfgang Grulke, as he spent a year being mentored, learning how to put presentations together, connect with global clients and manage a small IP-based business. That was then extended by nine wonderful years with a few business partners, who stretched him and developed his relational abilities. He has also found inspiration and support in the Global Federation of Professional Speakers, an industry body that he is involved in.

A 'room with a view' usually involves a person who may not call himself a mentor but who helps you to see beyond the current reality to something more. We believe that mentoring holds the key for progress and development for you and for many others. You want to find yourself a mentor who can help to stretch you to see beyond the current reality. Surround yourself with people who demand more from you and who push you to your limits.

WHAT THIS MEANS FOR YOU

If there is one word which should stand out in your mind in connection with this stage, it is *persistence*. There is no possibility of 'something for nothing'. Making your ideas into a reality requires unyielding and persistent effort. Remain focused on your definite aim, choose powerfully and continually take small steps towards achieving your chief definite aim.

COACHES' CORNER

If you want to remain on track and make it happen, we suggest forming the habit of focusing your mind on your definite aim and identifying questions you need to answer in order to move closer to that definite aim. Your mind will start to look for the answers and, surprisingly, as your mind focuses on the solutions, you will find answers and be able to move forward.

Tanya identified the following questions that she needed to answer in order to step closer to her definite aim:

- Who is giving this therapy? And how can I contact them?
- What do I need to study to be able to provide art therapy?
- What are the benefits of art therapy?
- Do I have sufficient time and money to learn to do it?
- What post-operative care centres exist?
- Are they financially successful?

We also suggest signing up to a goal-tracking service and receiving all the goal reminders and reporting you desire. Various options include:

- Lifetick (www.lifetick.com)
- Mindbloom Life Game (www.mindbloom.com)
- Goalscape (www.goalscape.com)
- Milestone Planner (www.milestoneplanner.com)

Finally, try to read the Brazen Life blog (www.brazenlife.com) on a regular basis.

MAIN POINTS

Making it happen involves clarifying an idea into a definite aim through information gathering and reflection and creating opportunities through networking strategies.

Choosing powerfully involves making a choice to commit all your resources to making one idea a reality and closing the door on other competing ideas.

Establishing a set of questions that need to be answered on a regular basis will help to keep your brain focused on the definite aim and be less likely to be distracted by an easier or safer option.

SUGGESTED READING

Paradox of Choice by Barry Schwartz (Harper Perennial, 2004)
Connected by Nicholas A Christakis and James H Fowler (Little, Brown and Company, 2009)
What Color is your Parachute? by Richard N Bolles (Ten Speed Press, 2010)
Synchronicity: The Inner Path of Leadership by Joseph Jaworski (Berrett-Koehler, 1998)

7

STAGE 5: STAYING ON TOP OF YOUR GAME

'The indispensable employee brings humanity and connection and art to her organization. She is the key player, the one who's difficult to live without, the person you can build something around.'
Seth Godin in Linchpin

'It is a remarkable feature of our times that so many are willing to forego their right to design their own futures.'
Ashis Nandy

Finally, you've reached the last stage of the Career Navigation Model. Hopefully, you've followed our advice and have used this book as a workbook, completing each of the tasks and activities we've recommended. Even if you haven't yet fully realised your career ambitions, you can begin to visualise them, and you should be excited about achieving career success.

There's one final step for you to complete. And it's a big one.

CONSTANTLY DEVELOP YOURSELF

The world of work is so fast-moving these days that even just to stand still, you've got to keep moving forward. To put it another way, because of all the changes taking place around you and the growing complexity of the new world of work, if you stop developing yourself – if you stop looking for opportunities to advance your career and to grow as a person – you will quickly be considered 'stale', out of date and yesterday's star.

Stage 5 of the Career Navigation Model is 'Staying on Top of Your Game'. A sport reference should help you to develop a mental picture. Think of any sport you enjoy and consider what happens when one person or team has a dominating season and beats all the competition. They become the target, the benchmark, the new standard of how things should be done. They are almost never able to sustain this for more than another season or two before others catch up, copy them and then overtake them. If that individual or team rests on their laurels and simply relies on past successes, they quickly lose their winning ways.

Some of the careers that you might choose are competitive and this analogy is then particularly apt for you. But even if there is no real competition for, or within your job, it is still important for you to stay fresh, committed, relevant and engaged for as long as your career might last. And as we saw in Chapter 4, that might be a lot longer than you initially thought.

There's also a good psychological reason to keep improving yourself: it's part of our nature as human beings to want to improve ourselves. The more you do this, the easier it will become. You definitely want to make developing yourself a habit.

So Stage 5 is not just a once-off activity that you do and tick off your list. What we're actually suggesting is that you change your mindset about what it means to have a career and that you set yourself up to stay successful for the rest of your life, regardless of how the world changes and shifts around you. In Chapter 2, we outlined some of the ways the world could change, but no one can tell for sure what will happen in the next decade, or the one after that – and you can't anticipate everything that could happen to you personally either. Your final task, therefore, as a career navigator is to be preparing yourself constantly for whatever might come your way. You should always be improving yourself and becoming the very best you that you can be.

HAVE AN ANNUAL CAREER CHECK-UP

Most people think about their jobs every day but don't take that much time out to think about their *careers*. You've been doing that as you've worked through this book, and hopefully it's helped you to get a really great job. But it would be the wrong thing to stop thinking about your career now. Keep the Self-Q test somewhere where you can see it and make sure that your career goals are written out and visible, so that there are constant reminders of where you're heading.

Take time once a year (January is a good time) to take yourself out for lunch or coffee and write down how you're feeling about your career. What makes you happy, and what would you like to change? Is your current job really what you want to be doing? Is it everything you hoped for? Or, at the least, is it helping you to reach your life and career goals (your definite aim from Stage 4)?

You can also do some specific job-related research. Is your income in line with your field and position? If you're in a large company, do some research on what opportunities might be available for you – to be promoted, moved or developed. Consider options for taking on new responsibilities, updating skills, working towards a promotion or starting to look out for that next position.

In Chapter 2, we talked about working *on* your business and not *in* your business. This is what a career check-up is: working *on* your career and not just *in* your career. Just as you might do a health check-up on your physical body, think of this process as an annual check-up for your career health. If you feel good about everything, that's great! If there are things that could be improved, think about how you can fix them in the year ahead.

DO A BETTER JOB

This book has been about developing your career and not just a specific job. But one of the best ways to keep developing your career is to make sure you do the very best job you can do in the position you're in now. One of the best ways to do that is to over-deliver on expectations and be more productive.

There are plenty of techniques available to help you become more productive. Read up on time blocking, the Pomodoro Technique (www.pomodorotechnique.com), the productivity tools listed at http://lifedev.net/big-list-of-online-productivity-tools, or anything on www.workawesome.com. Different people need to take different approaches; however you do it, there will be some method or technique that will work for you, and help you to save time, be more organised, streamline a process or get things done in a better way. Our suggestion is to try at least four new productivity techniques this year and see what works for you.

10 000 hours

A lot of research has been put into the subject of talent and maximising abilities. Malcom Gladwell suggested in his book, *Outliers: The Story of Success* (Penguin Books, 2009), that if you want to be a world expert on anything, you need to put 10 000 hours of effort into developing yourself and gaining experience. The theory emerged from Anders Ericsson's research among students at the Berlin Academy of Music in the 1990s. The students were divided into different groups, based on their musical excellence, and their practice patterns and history were analysed. The top performers had all put in over 10 000 hours of practice. The lowest ranked performers had all practised less than 4 000 hours. Gladwell provides many other examples, from the Beatles to Bill Gates, showing that the '10 000-hour Rule' is one of the secrets to success in any field.

Manie Bosman of Strategic Leadership Institute (www.strategicleadership institute.net) argues that, although anyone could probably become fairly good at just about anything if they're willing to practise for 10 000 hours, 'we only excel and become really expert if we spend those hours honing our natural talents into strengths or, in the case of natural geniuses, super-strengths'. He continues that not everyone's talents can become super-strengths: '... Some people just naturally have "stronger" talents than others. Can everyone attain some level of extraordinary success by discovering and developing their natural talents through practice and training? Yes, I believe so with my heart and soul.'

DEVELOP YOUR 'X-FACTORS'

In order to develop and grow your career, you need to stand out from the crowd. It's important that you keep developing the skills and attitudes that show you understand the changes taking place in the world around you, and are keeping up-to-date and ahead of the pack.

In his best-selling previous book, *Future-proof Your Child: Parenting the Wired Generation* (Penguin Books, 2008), Graeme and his co-author, Nikki Bush, suggested that parents of today's children should be helping them to develop five 'X-factors'. These often difficult-to-define attributes are key to standing out from the crowd in the 21st century world of work. There's no reason that you can't develop them too, even as an adult. They are:

Breaking conventions (creativity)

A key defining factor of talented people, in any industry or arena, is their ability to break conventions, push boundaries and stretch the limits of performance. This can be learnt by deliberately developing creativity, imagination and innovative thinking, as well as taking the time to play more, putting yourself in unusual situations and asking more questions about the world around you. Be curious.

Being resilient

This is successful adaptation to risk and adversity, which includes the critical skill of being able to change and be adaptable. A never-give-up attitude is typical of those who are identified as talented. They are actually quick to give up on things they know they're not good at and unbelievably tenacious in those things they want to succeed at. Sticking to the task at hand teaches self-discipline, commitment and delayed gratification, and is what we covered in the last chapter when we talked about making a choice.

Learning

A love of learning, in addition to the skills and competencies required to learn, will be amongst the most important characteristics you can develop to ensure that you remain continually relevant – as well as continually intrigued and engaged by life. Regardless of what life throws at you, if you are willing and eager to learn, you will be able to work out how to cope. This requires curiosity and focus, as well as an ability to process information and filter it too.

Knowing yourself

Self-awareness refers to knowing your internal states, preferences, resources and intuitions. Jonathan Cook, a psychologist at the Gordon Institute of Business Science, has identified three important components of self-awareness: emotional awareness (recognising your emotions and their effects), accurate self-assessment (knowing your strengths and limits), and self-confidence (a strong sense of your self-worth and capabilities). We dealt with this extensively in Stage 1 of the Career Navigation Model. Your goal in this final stage is to keep your personal profile updated, as you develop new skills, change some attitudes and gain experience.

Relating to others

Daniel Goleman refers to 'social intelligence' and Howard Gardner to 'interpersonal intelligence' in labelling the competencies that determine how we handle relationships with others. Each of these researchers stresses two overarching categories of social competence: empathy and social skills. This involves skills relating to communication, collaboration, teamwork, comfort with diversity and networking (which we dealt with in the previous chapter).

CREATE AND CONSTANTLY UPDATE A PERSONAL DEVELOPMENT PLAN

Developing yourself, whether it's putting in 10 000 hours, focusing on your strengths or developing X-factors, is most effective when using a specific, formal plan. You should aim to add a few development items each year. Sometimes it's about learning something new. Other times, it can be about unlearning or deciding to stop doing something else.

You don't only need to think about a development plan when you're looking for a job. Even if you're not adding a new job to your résumé this year, you can still add to the other sections. Are there technical skills that would make you more competitive in your field? Are there attitudes you need to change? Are there tools that could make your job (or your boss's or colleagues' jobs) easier? Can you attend a training course or management class that would better position you for a promotion?

For inspiration, have a look at the LinkedIn profiles of your colleagues who are a step or two higher than you, and think about how you can add their areas of expertise to your own skills set.

Note that you can't just sit back and hope that these development opportunities will somehow come your way. You need to go and look for them. The manager of external graduate programmes at Deloitte explained to us that employees are required to *pull* learning and development opportunities towards themselves as opposed to the way it was done previously, when companies pushed the opportunities on to the employees. Clearly some *push* still occurs for essential business competencies and skills. But most employers now require staff to *pull* the resources and skills they need, just when they need them. So career navigators will need to decide what and when to pull certain opportunities – it's up to you.

Kagiso

Kagiso was seeking ideas that would allow him to be engaged. He arranged interviews, did online research and had coffee with many people in his network. More knowledge and understanding came his way as he progressed through his career, allowing him to make more connections and arrive at more ideas. This is natural and quite expected. Becoming engaged in the workplace does take some trial and error, learning and questioning. After spending time in the Theatre of Dreams, Kagiso created this ideas sheet:

Kagiso identified these questions to stay on track:

In what area or role could I use my 'ideation' and 'futuristic' talents?
What is the difference between business and product development?
What are the role possibilities from within the bank or elsewhere?
What are the interim steps to securing these roles?

What skill and knowledge do I require to secure those roles?

What makes a person in that role excellent?

Where are my gaps? Can I expect to fill the gaps?

What salaries/bonuses do they pay?

Who in product development could I speak to?

Kagiso identified the questions he had not yet answered and then put in place a plan to obtain those answers. This plan included making time with the HR manager, speaking to his mentor, speaking to the lecturer at the business school. He knew he needed to take responsibility for his own career and make use of the support around him to find the best way forward for him.

After significant action in this stage, he created this personal development plan to guide his short term steps.

Personal Development Plan			Timeframe	Measure of Success/Method for Tracking Progress
CURRENT POSITION		• Completed graduate programme • Rotation throughout bank divisions		
DESIRED SHORT-TERM ROLE		• Product development manager	12 – 18 months	Promotion awarded
REQUIREMENTS FOR SHORT-TERM ROLE	SKILLS	• Financial analysis and projections • Market and market trends analysis • Budgeting and forecasting • ROI analysis • Product design • Business report writing		
	NEEDED KNOWLEDGE	• Product knowledge • Competitors' product knowledge • Industry understanding		
	OTHER REQUIREMENTS	• Relationships with product team and sales/marketing team		

Personal Development Plan		Timeframe	Measure of Success/Method for Tracking Progress
ACTION PLAN TO OBTAIN MISSING SKILLS, KNOWLEDGE & OTHER REQUIREMENTS	<ul><li>On-the-job experience (see below)</li><li>Reading and research on all products becoming a product expert</li><li>Obtain training on the available computer tools and programmes</li><li>Attend learning programme at business school to gain more understanding of financial management and analysis.</li><li>Obtain training on business and report-writing skills</li></ul>		
INTERIM ROLES FOR EXPERIENCE	<ul><li>Product development assistant OR</li><li>Product development co-ordinator</li></ul>		
DESIRED LONGER-TERM ROLE	<ul><li>Consulting on product development</li></ul>	5 – 10 years	Performing that role
REQUIREMENTS FOR LONG-TERM ROLE	SKILLS	<ul><li>Creation of product plans</li><li>Option comparisons</li><li>Financial analysis</li><li>Communication skills</li><li>Presentation skills</li><li>Client management skills</li><li>Meeting management skills</li><li>Report-writing skills</li><li>Negotiation skills</li></ul>	
	NEEDED KNOWLEDGE	<ul><li>Competitor offerings</li><li>Client needs and business issues</li><li>Previous product offerings with their success and failures</li></ul>		
	OTHER REQUIREMENTS	<ul><li>Presentation skills</li><li>Building reputation and brand</li><li>Networking</li><li>Reliable suppliers</li></ul>		

Personal Development Plan		Timeframe	Measure of Success/Method for Tracking Progress
ACTION PLAN TO OBTAIN NEEDED SKILLS, KNOWLEDGE & OTHER REQUIREMENTS	• MBA at business school • Coaching on communicating more effectively • Practise writing skills • Practise meeting-management skills • Training on conflict management • Manage reputation		
INTERIM ROLES FOR EXPERIENCE	• Identify consulting role models and watch and learn • Attend sales meeting to learn about negotiation		

UPDATE YOUR RÉSUMÉ AND PROFILES

Keeping your résumé up-to-date is vital for several reasons. If a recruiter calls you out of the blue with a great job opportunity, you'll want to have an updated document ready to go. In the digital space, every time you do an update, your online bio is refreshed and re-indexed. This can get you noticed. While you're getting your paper résumé in shape, go through the rest of your documents and all your digital profiles to refresh your portfolio.

STRETCH AND CHALLENGE YOURSELF

Depending on where you are in your career, you might just want to take a few months to settle in and enjoy your life for a while. Don't get too complacent or comfortable, but recognise that you don't have to jump from job to job, as long as you keep growing and developing.

Try to be involved in identifying and securing career-enhancing opportunities, such as stretch assignments, interesting projects, cross-functional on-the-job experience, working at companies that provide good learning and development opportunities, or simply volunteering to do a job that's daunting for you.

You may want to identify a variety of role models who show particular strengths, such as a person who communicates well in meetings, continually develops himself, writes exceptional meeting notes or is excellent at holding crucial conversations. A role model can open your eyes to what is possible in daily interactions and activities as well as in the long term.

EXPAND YOUR NETWORK

Contrary to popular belief, the best time to network isn't when you're looking for a job – it's long before then. There's a simple reason for this: having a broad and diverse network already in place will make your job search easier. Now is the time to be active in building your network of contacts and career supporters.

Before you complain that you hate networking, remember that there are many ways to make new connections and strengthen existing ones. You don't have to get stuck at networking lunches every other day. You could ask your company to send you on a conference that looks interesting; connect with a colleague who has left and gone to another business, or, at the very least, join some LinkedIn groups and do your networking in the digital world.

Try to meet at least one new person every month and you'll have a dozen new contacts by this time next year!

STOP AND UNLEARN

One of the most powerful tools for learning in the 21st century is the concept of *un*learning. It's quite easy to identify new skills, information or attitudes that you might need to learn, but it's another altogether to try to identify those things within yourself that are no longer useful or helpful. These might be habits, actions, attitudes or even relationships that you have should firmly place in the bin of your history. Let them go and unlearn.

What do you need to unlearn? Go on, take a few minutes and make a list.

DEVELOP TRANSFERABLE SKILLS

It is highly likely that you will change jobs and industries during your career. You want to have obtained and developed skills that can be used in a variety of companies and across industries.

KEEP YOUR EYES ON THE HORIZON

The best career navigators, while doing all they can to choose to be content and focused on the job they've decided to pursue, still keep an eye on the future. You should keep up-to-date with developments in your field and know what's happening in the world around you.

The Institute for the Future is a non-profit research centre focused on long-term forecasting. In 2011, they released a report titled 'Future Work Skills 2020' (available at www.iftf.org/futureworkskills2020) that analyses some of the key drivers that are reshaping work. They then suggest 10 key skills for the future of work. This list would be good for you to check against your Self-Q test and your personal development plan, to ensure you're not missing an important future skill.

There are many other ways to keep an eye on the future. For example, most business magazines have one annual edition focused on the future of work. Many business books and personal development books can also help you on your path.

WHAT THIS MEANS FOR YOU

The reason for doing all of this work is to help you not only to find a job for the rest of your life, but to give you an abiding sense of calm about your ability to create and develop your career no matter what happens to the job you're in right now.

There is a need for career navigators to learn continually, with the goal of ongoing relevance and lifetime employability.

COACHES' CORNER

- Create a personal development plan.
- Appoint a friend or mentor to monitor your progress in line with your personal development plan.
- You will need to update your personal development plan regularly to take slight changes in direction and interest into account.

MAIN POINTS

There is a need for career navigators to continually learn, with the goal of ongoing relevance and lifetime employability.

In order to achieve lifetime employability and relevance, you need to stay on top of your game. The following are suggested actions for doing this:

- Constantly develop yourself.
- Have an annual career check-up.
- Do a better job.
- Develop your X-factors.
- Create and constantly update a Personal Development Plan.
- Update your résumé and profiles.
- Stretch and challenge yourself.
- Expand your network.
- Develop transferable skills.
- Stop and unlearn.
- Keep your eyes on the horizon.

SUGGESTED READING

What got you here, won't get you there by Marshall Goldsmith (Profile Books, 2008)

Mojo by Marshall Goldsmith (Profile Books, 2010)

StandOut by Marcus Buckingham (Thomas Nelson, 2011)

8

OVERCOMING COMMON CHALLENGES

You know now that career navigation is not a task that you can ever tick off your to-do list. To do it properly requires working at it every day for the rest of your working life. Once you're over the initial hurdle of finding your ideal job and knowing your career path, you need to maintain your balance and focus, and ensure that you stay as fulfilled as you can be.

Of course, you know that this is not as easy as it might sound, and requires a lot of effort and energy. There might be some challenges that threaten to derail or confuse you. Here are some of the most common issues that career navigators have to deal with, as well as some important additional information to help you stay on track – not just for now, but for the rest of your working life.

MONEY AND BEING ENGAGED

'I would like to enjoy my work but I have to make money.' This statement reflects a common mindset and can easily trap you in your current position. In fact, it is this perception – that they can't leave their current jobs because they need the money – that prevents many people from even trying to become engaged and fulfilled. We propose that you seek to be engaged before seeking money, as we believe that being engaged generates significantly more rewards and recognition in the longer term. When you are chasing money *and* you are not engaged, you become one of the crowd – average, money-grabbing, lacking in depth and 100% replaceable.

Trying to increase income or find a quick-fix solution, without first focusing on what you know about yourself is unlikely to lead to long-term success.

Kevin was a rugby-watching, beer-drinking, average South African man of 35. His buddy of many years, Tim, presented him with an opportunity to go into an IT venture. Tim told him that it involved the latest and greatest products and 'was sure to be a winner'. Kevin had to do all the sales, which, according to Tim 'would be easy, as they really just sell themselves'.

So Kevin (whose Self-Q Tool showed an analytical, reserved man with experience and interest in mechanical engineering) became the salesman for IT products because the venture was a 'sure winner'. He pursued the opportunity, ignoring everything he had discovered about himself and it took eight months before he came back. Sheepishly, he arrived at Kerry's office and said, 'You know, all that stuff you told me about me was right. In sales, the telephone rings all day, with people asking questions and wanting demos. It makes me crazy. I don't get to sit and think anymore as I have to run around selling products. It drains me.'

There are very few 'sure winners' out there that don't involve hard work and persistence. As soon as hard work is required, you need to remember what you learnt about yourself in your Self-Q tool to maximise your chance of success.

If you do choose to take a job that is not in line with your Self-Q tool, identify the likely consequences of your choice so you can recognise the consequences when they arise and you don't become despondent. Use them to propel you into action to achieve satisfaction in the longer term.

If you are engaged, you will be prepared to work more, for longer hours, overcoming challenges and doing what needs to be done. This may well be why being engaged leads to greater financial rewards.

In the short term, financial responsibilities may make it difficult to make a significant career change to be engaged and fulfilled. It is, however, possible to start to carve yourself a more suitable role. Seek training and development opportunities, volunteer for suitable projects and take steps (even baby steps) to become more engaged in the longer term. Use your current situation to develop skills, contacts and knowledge that can help you make a move to a career that is more fulfilling and in line with your Self-Q tool. You need to change your mindset to see your current job as a stepping stone, rather than a holding pen. The biggest danger you face is getting stuck in a job that pays the bills but isn't what you want to do with your life.

You may also consider temporarily downgrading your lifestyle so that you can reduce costs and earn less. You may even be able to save a lot in a short space of time. Both of these options would temporarily allow you to accept less money as you pursue the dream job that will allow you to be engaged.

Career navigators want to put their greed and materialism aside and make choices to find fulfilment and satisfaction. If career navigators choose jobs for the money alone, it is likely they will receive only money. They will have no one to blame for that outcome except themselves.

CHOOSING BETWEEN TWO (OR MORE) OPTIONS

Frequently career navigators ask, 'How do I choose between two or more opportunities?'

Ideally, career navigators should have the courage to follow their hearts and intuition. However, many people facing a career dilemma are overcome by anxiety, responsibility and fear. They are either unable to identify what their hearts are saying, or they are scared to follow its advice.

Dr John Demartini, in his book, *Inspired Destiny* (Hay House, 2010), noted that every option has equal positives and negatives. You may not be able to see them but if you really look, they are there. So when you are making a choice between two or more options, you are seeking to choose the one that is most in line with your values and most in line with your life goals. He explains that in your areas of highest value, you are likely to have the greatest amount of attention, focus, discipline and dedication, making it more possible to achieve your goals.

Bearing this in mind, we have created three brief tests, which can help you to identify the most suitable option. Take each career option through these tests and answer each question with 'no', 'moderately' or 'yes'. A 'no' answer in any of these tests is like an alarm bell warning you of danger. There are likely to be negative consequences of choosing this option in the short or longer term.

Test 1: The Self-Q tool

Do your Self-Q tool results support this option? That is, does the option meet your work preferences? Does it make use of some of your talents? Is it in line with your career anchor identified in the Self-Q tool?

If you go against the patterns and preferences identified in the Self-Q tool, you can expect to suffer some consequences. It may be frustration; it may be that you aren't promoted as others are better at the role than you; it may be boredom. You go against it at your peril.

Test 2: Options value

Does the option provide you with career enhancement? That is, will it open doors and opportunities for you or will it provide learning opportunities which will open up many opportunities?

The new world of work requires a career navigator to keep learning and developing. Choosing an option that will involve career advancement and not career enhancement can limit your future prospects as your skills may become outdated.

Test 3: Delicious

Does this option feel enticing, enchanting, exciting and exhilarating? You are seeking an opportunity that feels delicious. An opportunity that will allow you to be engaged is likely to spark something inside you. If fear, your ego, greed or family expectations are driving you towards an option, it is unlikely to feel delicious.

You will spend a large portion of your life at work. You want to be engaged and find fulfilment in your work. People who experience career success and fulfilment require a 'yes' to this question.

Remember John from Chapter 1, who had two job opportunities in his current company and was also considering starting his own consulting business as a third option. His Self-Q tool is shown overleaf.

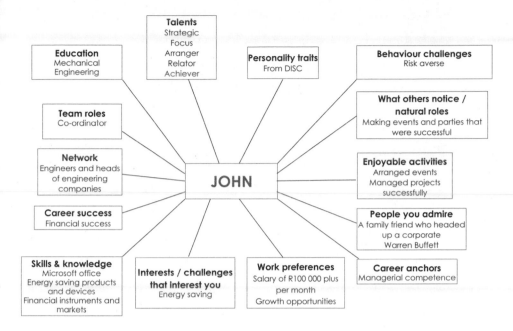

John applied the three tests, considering his options carefully. Option 1 involved managing a team of people on an energy-saving project. Option 2 was a more technical role, getting involved in designing products for energy saving. Option 3 was to start his own consulting business on energy-saving devices.

Test 1: The Self-Q tool

Options 1 and 2 met his work preferences by providing growth opportunities and a salary in excess of R100 000 per month. If he was to set up his own business, it would take some time before he would receive such a large salary but there may be the possibility of building value that could be realised in the future. This may have been a good reason to compromise on work preferences.

His career anchor showed that managerial competence was his main driver, as opposed to technical and functional competence. This supported Option 1 but not Option 2.

He was also risk averse. He wanted to make good money without having to take too much risk. Starting his own business at this stage would involve significant risk and he felt it was not a good time.

Result: Option 1 was 'yes' and Options 2 and 3 were 'no'.

Test 2: Options value

Option 1 and Option 2 would open up many opportunities to John. They will both ensure career enhancement in the form of new learning and contacts. His own business, if successful, would open up more opportunities for him but it would significantly reduce options if it failed.

Result: all three options were 'yes'.

Test 3: Delicious

John enjoyed managing projects, particularly those with energy-saving goals. In this position, he could use his 'arranger' and 'relater' talents. The project would require him to evaluate options to choose the best way forward, which would involve using his 'strategic' talent. He felt good about the role, knowing he could be engaged.

Result: Option 1 was 'yes'. Option 2 was 'moderately' and Option 3 was 'no'.

It was clear from these tests that Option 1 was the preferred option and he could make his choice with confidence. Choosing between options can be a daunting and difficult task, and there are no easy answers. Sometimes you just have to choose and believe you've made the right decision. If you haven't, you will be able to change things at a later stage. These three tests are simple but very helpful in making these choices.

Career enhancement, not career advancement

If your options include one prestigious option and others that are more in line with your career aspirations, you may feel that this is a difficult choice. It shouldn't be. Career navigators should always choose career enhancement as opposed to career advancement. They want to seek roles that open opportunities for more training and skills development. They should ignore roles that offer nothing much more than prestige, improved titles or position.

After working for a year in solving system problems, Kagiso faced a further dilemma: choosing between two job options. In the one role, he would be a project manager, but, as he said, 'the job will be just a job'. In the second role, he would not have the title of project manager but he would have interesting work and would be given many learning and development opportunities. He was considering taking the first role because he wanted to reach the top quickly. After reading about the new world of work and the need to keep growing and learning, he saw the value of choosing the second role, even if it meant accepting a lower salary and status in the short term, as it would ensure he would remain relevant in the longer term.

CAN I CHANGE? OR MUST I JUST ACCEPT WHO I AM?

Some career navigators want to take on roles that they are not ideally suited for. Their dreams exceed the abilities, their profiles or their potential.

When we did the Self-Q tool with Simon, he was not happy with what he saw. In fact he stormed out of Kerry's office. He wanted to be a strategic guru and the patterns that emerged indicated that he was better suited to operations management. All was quiet for a couple of weeks and just when Kerry had given up, she took a call late one Friday afternoon from Simon. He asked a simple question, 'So can I change?'

Career navigators do, in fact, need to change to improve skills, knowledge and education levels to keep up with the rapidly changing workplace. They also need to change to improve their workplace behaviour and reputation. They want to be able to accept the reality of a demanding boss or a failed tender bid or upcoming retirement.

On the other hand, while you can expand your vision of what is possible for yourself, you don't want the effort to get to the top to be too great and be heading up a sand dune that keeps sliding down around you. To put it another way, there are some things that can be changed and many things that can be learnt, but some of who you are is fixed. It's important to know what can be changed and what can't.

Simon wanted to change his thinking patterns and perceptions. To do this, he needed to focus more on the parts of himself that were good and that he saw value in, and focus less on trying to correct his weaknesses. Marcus Buckingham taught this in his book *Now Discover Your Strengths* (Pocket Books, 2001), saying that 'you will excel only by maximising your strengths, never by fixing your weaknesses'.

Simon had seen his patterns in the Self-Q tool and, afterwards, his patterns in his work. He noticed that his strategic ideas were quite average. He noticed that he was excellent at spotting what wasn't working and finding ways to make it more efficient. He excelled at operations management. Simon decided to focus on developing his natural thought patterns and invested in his excellence.

Career navigators also want to avoid becoming a square peg in a round hole. Stuart sold pension products, as they paid more commission than other insurance products. He was an excellent, well-connected salesman who entertained the clients at social functions with ease and grace. But his sales figures were low. He said to us that his clients always complimented him on his presentations but they didn't buy from him. He decided to ask one of the clients for some feedback. The client gave him a friendly pat on the back and said to him, 'We all think you are great and your presentations are the best. But, you know, this is our savings and, as we are responsible for other people's savings, we need to be cautious. Mr BB has been around for many years and has a reputation for being cautious and reliable. We feel safe with this option.'

Stuart's natural patterns were not suited to his role. People saw an entertaining salesman, not a safe pair of hands. He had to make a choice: either change himself or change his job. It would have been a mistake for him to squash his fun, entertaining nature and become a square peg in a round hole. We are glad to say he chose to sell exclusive property syndicate arrangements and he has done very well.

Excellence comes from accepting what you have been given and stretching yourself to be more of who you are already.

DOING WHAT YOU LOVE

One of the biggest challenges that career navigators face is settling for a job that they don't love. Many career navigators have to provide financially for their families and have to make responsible choices. However, they also have responsibilities to themselves and their levels of fulfilment.

Remember that your career affects so many aspects of your life including your health, wealth, self-esteem and relationships. As a career navigator, you have a responsibility to make sufficient money to pay the bills *and* be doing some or all of what you love (or at least be working on a plan to do what you love). A miserable dad or mom will negatively impact the family and community, just as much a poor cash balance.

Philip, for example, wanted to develop people and his Self-Q tool supported this desire. But he felt that he was being irresponsible by following his heart, as he really needed to pay the bills for his family. This is a familiar career dilemma, where fear and uncertainty generally trap the career navigator. For Philip, a role in learning and development felt 'delicious' and he wanted to pursue it to escape from a future in accounting. However he felt nervous and unsure, and he kept thinking of the bills he needed to pay. These are familiar concerns for people facing a career dilemma and choosing between what they would *love* to do and the perceived safer option. So what now?

DEVELOP YOUR UNIQUE SELLING PROPOSITION

One way to resolve some of the anxiety in following your heart is to seek to identify or build a unique selling proposition (USP) in doing what you love. If a career navigator has a USP in doing what he loves, he may feel comfortable (and responsible) in following his heart. It helps to ensure that your love can be financially viable and is not a hobby.

A USP is also useful for those seeking to maximise themselves. Note that building a USP is not building a Plan B; it is a Plan A with rocket fuel.

A company creates a unique selling proposition for its products to ensure that the product generates a profit for the company. A USP is a clear statement of what makes the company different from every other company, and can include multiple elements (such as different products, different prices, different distribution, different quality, and so on). Obviously, this difference indicates being better than the other companies.

As a career navigator, you should create a unique selling proposition by combining various elements (including your talents, experience, knowledge and attitudes) in a way that makes you unique. The career navigator who most uniquely suits the role will secure the job. The career navigator whose unique and irreplaceable skills help the organisation the most can command the highest rewards.

For each opportunity, take the following steps:

- Determine the characteristics and competencies that are valued for the position you are interested in. Step into the employer's or client's shoes and attempt to understand what they need and what they value.
- Compare your skills and competencies against a person who is successful in this role or field. From this you will be able to identify your strengths and weaknesses for this option.
- Look again at your Self-Q tool and highlight the parts of your profile that best match the key requirements of the opportunity.

Based on this analysis, develop your USP statement for this opportunity or create a plan for creating your USP (this will also assist you in an interview or any job discussion). The ideal job choice for you is one in which you will have a sustainable USP.

COPING SKILLS

Many career navigators become stressed and anxious and resort to a variety of remedies to cope. There is no doubt that a person needs to be strong, face up to the challenges and develop coping skills to deal with the very turbulent waters found in the new world of work.

Zandile, who participated on a corporate graduate programme, came to see us because she was not coping in her job. She had all the technical skills and, until recently, her performance on the job was good. She was anxiously waiting to hear if she had a permanent position. This stress was making her sick and unable to perform adequately. She became very unreliable and missed a deadline that negatively affected her chances of securing a permanent position.

You need to develop self-awareness so that you notice when you are becoming stressed and overburdened. Develop personal strategies to help you cope. These may include more sleep, more exercise, a walk in a quiet place, a massage or meditation, a beer or seeing friends, playing with the dog or listening to music. It really doesn't matter what it is as long as it provides you with the energy and strength you need to face the challenges again.

Through better self-management, Zandile did find the strength within to face her challenges head on. She did, in time, secure a permanent job and was able to continue to be reliable in her work.

NEVER SAY, 'IT'S NOT FAIR.'

If you're battling to find a job, or battling *in* your job, one of the simplest ways to justify your difficult circumstances is to blame the world. 'It's not fair,' you will say.

Conan O'Brien, an American comedian and talk show host, spoke in front of the graduating 2011 Dartmouth class. He was to the point as he said:

> My first job as your commencement speaker is to illustrate that life is not fair. You have worked tirelessly for four years to earn the diploma you'll be receiving this weekend. That was great. And Dartmouth is giving me the same degree for interviewing the fourth lead in *Twilight*. Deal with it. I have heard over and over again that the generation graduating today is continually called the 'entitled generation'. That they feel like they deserve the best jobs, the best pay, the best life. For some, it works out that way. But for most of us, we learned pretty quickly life isn't as forgiving and generous as we might have hoped. I think the best preparation for the 'real world' is a realistic understanding that it's much tougher than it used to be.

Our simple advice is never to allow yourself to say that life isn't fair. It might not be, but there's nothing you can do about it. Use what you've learnt in this book to make the most of what you have. Don't be a victim.

NEVER SAY, 'I'VE TRIED TO LOOK FOR A JOB AND CAN'T FIND ANYTHING.'

The Internet has been a massive help to those seeking jobs but has also created as many problems as it has solved. You can submit job applications to hundreds of firms very quickly – but so can everyone else! You cannot search for jobs just by submitting application after application. Frustrated job seekers often complain that they've submitted their résumé hundreds of times online with no response. Of course, the Internet is a fairly good source of information about opportunities, but online applications are not a good basis for a job-seeking strategy.

The best strategy has multiple approaches, including applying online, listing your résumé at job portals, working through your network, attending networking events, making new connections, doing informational interviews, making physical applications, using social media in your job search, and improving your personal profile online. There's no quick-fix solution. You have to try everything – or as much as you can – because you just don't know which strategy will pay off. Our experience shows that you really do need to get out from your computer screen, though. Online is not enough.

We think that one of the easiest, but most effective strategies for job seekers is to let as many people as possible know you're looking for a job. We realise that there might be times when you need to keep your job hunt a bit quiet (for example, if you don't want your existing employer to know just yet that you're looking for a new job), but even then, there are probably at least a few people in your network – former colleagues, friends, family, mentors, online connections – who you could tell. When you do this, it's best to be as specific as you can be about what you're looking for. The more specific you are, the better other people will be able to help you. Tell people about the items on your Self-Q test, the types of opportunities that would interest you, and your career aspirations. Send them your résumé and ask that they keep you in mind if they hear of anything. Make sure that you keep your network informed and updated as your search progresses.

Ashley Hoffman, writing on the Brazen Careerist blog in January 2012, gave the following excellent advice:

> One of the best things you can do when you're job searching is find and connect with people who have a similar job to the one you want, work at a company you want to work for, or simply have great connections in your industry. An effective way to do this is through the informational interview.
>
>   How do you find these people? Ask your network (and ask them to make an intro for you), search on LinkedIn (and look for shared connections for the intro) or Facebook or Twitter for a start. Introduce yourself over email and give a quick 4-5 sentence reason why you're contacting them. Ask for

a meeting (ideally, if in the same city) or a phone call. ALWAYS make it convenient for them and put a time limit on the call.

Try saying something like, 'I'm sure you're really busy, but if you have 30 minutes in the next two weeks, I'd be interested in buying you a cup of coffee at a location convenient for you or stop by your office for a quick chat. I'd love to hear how you got started in the field/company X!'

Most people know the purpose of these meetings and many will be open to meeting with you. After all, people usually like to talk about themselves and work they enjoy.

When you're at the meeting, tell them about yourself and what you're looking for and then focus mainly on them, asking questions about what they do. The key to these meetings is to follow up; never send your résumé upfront unless they ask for it, but attach it in your thank you email with a note like, 'Great meeting with you and hearing about your experience in the field! I've attached my résumé to this email in case you do hear of any opportunities.' This person is now part of your network and you should do upkeep with this relationship as you do with any other.

IT DOESN'T HAVE TO END: RE-TYRE-MENT

We have argued throughout this book that the traditional career model is pretty much dead. A few people may finish studying, get a junior job in a big company and stay there until they retire at age 65, but this will very much be the exception these days. One of the biggest shifts about to happen is how we view retirement. Simply put, we think retirement is going to be retired.

In fact, we often have a chance to talk about retirement with people who are navigating their careers, and our message is very clear: very soon, it isn't going to look anything like it does today! That's great news for those of you reading this book who are a bit older. If you don't want to stop working, then don't. Reskill, retool, refire, retyre, but don't stop doing what you love. We use the term 're-tyre-ment' to help make our point. Just as you can take an old tyre and have it retreaded and patched up so that it can travel a few more thousand kilometres, so we believe that people can have their careers retreaded, or re-tyred, and be good to go for another few years, or even decades.

If you are nearing or already over the traditional retirement age of 65, then you might find real value in connecting with the excellent team from the Refirement Network (see www.refirementnetwork.com). They provide support and resources for those who wish to continue working after retirement, whether that is in your old industry or somewhere else.

COACHES' CORNER

- If you are struggling to cope: identify five activities or events that re-energise you and make a commitment to do three of them this week.
- If you are taking the victim role or saying life is not fair: notice your victim behaviour and attitudes. Identify three behaviours or attitudes that are needed to adopt the mindset of 'My career is my responsibility'.
- If you want to follow your passion: identify what need you will be meeting and who will be paying to have that need met. Identify what contribution you will be making and who is prepared to pay for that contribution.
- If you seek career enhancement (as opposed to career advancement): identify the best next step you can take to develop your skills. (So what is holding you back from taking it? Bet you it is your desire for a salary or title!)

MAIN POINTS

Seeking to be engaged before seeking money, recognition or any other form of reward is likely to lead to greater rewards in the longer term.

When struggling to make a choice between two or more options, consider three questions:

- Does the Self-Q tool support this option?
- Does this option open doors and learning opportunities?
- Does this option feel delicious?

Answering no to any of these questions should raise alarm bells that negative consequences may result.

As a career navigator, you should choose career enhancement as opposed to career advancement. You want to seek roles that open opportunities for more training and skill development. You should ignore roles that offer nothing much more than prestige, improved titles or position. Excellence comes from accepting what you have been given and stretching yourself to be more of who you are.

To increase the chances of being successful in doing what you love, complete a USP.

As career navigator, you need to develop self-awareness so that you notice when you are becoming stressed and overburdened. You need to develop personal strategies to help you cope and face the challenges head on.

Life is not fair and there is not much you can do about it. Use what you've learnt in this book to make the most of what you have. Don't be a victim.

The great news for older readers is that, if you don't want to stop working, you don't have to. Reskill, retool, refire, retyre, but don't stop doing what you love.

SUGGESTED READING

Inspired Destiny by Dr John F Demartini (Hay House, 2010)
The Empty Raincoat by Charles Handy (Arrow Books, 2002)

A BIT OF INSPIRATION

If I had my life to live over,
I'd try to make more mistakes next time.
I would relax. I would limber up.
I would be sillier than I have on this trip.
I would be crazier. I would be less hygienic.
I would take more chances, I would take more trips.
I would climb more mountains, swim more rivers, and watch more sunsets.
I would burn more gasoline. I would eat more ice cream and less beans.
I would have more actual troubles and fewer imaginary ones.
You see, I am one of those people who lives prophylactically and sensibly and sanely, hour after hour, day after day.

Oh, I have had my moments

And if I had it to do over again, I'd have more of them.

In fact, I'd try to have nothing else.

Just moments, one after another.

Instead of living so many years ahead each day.

I have been one of those people who never go anywhere without a thermometer, a hot water bottle, a gargle, a raincoat, and a parachute.

If I had to do it over again, I would go places and do things.

I'd travel lighter than I have.

If I had my life to live over, I would start barefooted earlier in the spring and stay that way later in the fall.

I would play hooky more. I wouldn't make such good grades except by accident.

I would ride on merry-go-rounds.

I'd pick more daisies!

Nadine Stair

IN CONCLUSION

'The road to success is dotted with many tempting parking spaces.'
Will Rogers

THE JOURNEY

Throughout this book, you've briefly connected with six people and shared some of their career navigation journeys. We're thrilled to tell you that, at the time of writing, Philip, Nicole, Kagiso, John, Tanya and Lutendo are all engaged and staying on top of their games. That doesn't mean they love every minute of every day of their jobs. It means they're now fulfilled, happy, motivated and contributing. Let's briefly look at their learning.

Philip adopted the mindset 'My career is my responsibility' and, by looking inward, was able to complete his Self-Q tool and identify his career drivers. This allowed him to seek more appropriate work in the new world of work that would allow him to be engaged. Using his network and improving his skill and knowledge, he secured himself a position heading up learning and development for an IT company.

Lutendo also learnt to take responsibility for his career and, by developing and, using job-hunting skills, secured a great job in a graphic design agency. He was surprised at how much effort it required but was thrilled with the outcome.

Nicole adopted the mindset 'I create career success' and combined her analytical talent with her desire to protect the monies of vulnerable people. She secured a job at the financial ombudsman and is now able to pay her monthly bills *and* find meaning in her daily work.

For Tanya, leaving full-time employment felt too big a first step, so we helped her to start the journey by using her free time to develop contacts skills and experience that might eventually lead to her dream of an art therapy centre. Sometimes big career moves can be made in small steps, as long as you don't lose sight of the final goal destination. Tanya adopted the mindset 'I learn'. She refused to view herself a failure but rather learnt from her experience. She looked for ways to meet her career drivers more effectively.

Kagiso adopted the mindset 'I seek to be engaged'. He kept one eye on his personal development plan and one eye on his level of engagement. He continually looked for ways to meet his career drivers more effectively and, in so doing, become more engaged and effective.

John learnt some effective questions to ask when trying to make a choice between job options. More importantly, he learnt that his career planning needed to be more than making a series of short-term job choices.

NOW IT IS YOUR TURN

The route is now laid out in front of you. Your new mindsets ensure that you are in the driver's seat, believing you can achieve career success and always seeking to learn. What remains is to manage your expectations about this journey.

If you look at the path of any successful career navigator, you will see effort and perseverance. You will also find that almost no career navigators have achieved this alone. Like most great journeys, your career navigation will be better if shared with others. Involve your family and friends, your network and anyone you can as you choose your future and work towards it. *Work* is what you will need to do. Sadly, there doesn't seem to be a shortcut to success.

The journey you are about to embark on will demand everything you have available to you. But that is okay, as this journey may be what defines your life. This is your chance to make a contribution, to make a difference and to be more than you ever dreamt possible. This is your chance to escape the Trap that holds so many people back.

The great news is that it's up to you and you can start right now. In fact, you already have.wWe would love to hear about your journey. Send us an email on kerry@patwork.co.za.

Good luck!

ACKNOWLEDGEMENTS

Kerry:

Thank you to Graeme who has calmly steered this book to completion and has stepped in with his professional touch just when it was most needed. I am very grateful to you, Graeme for sharing your insights on the new world of work and for expressing your viewpoint so beautifully. You are a wonderful role model to fellow career navigators and I thank you for agreeing to this collaboration and assisting me to guide and support fellow career navigators.

To Andrew, without whom this book would not have been possible. Your ideas, comments, suggestions and mostly your honesty is invaluable. You continue to open our eyes to new possibilities and new ways of seeing the ordinary. I always look forward to your next big idea and wish you so much success as you navigate your career.

To each and every career navigator who has been brave enough to consult with me and in so doing has helped me to refine the career navigation process. I have learnt so much from each and every one of you and a huge thank you goes out to all of you. I look forward to working with many more career navigators and further refining the process as we all seek to navigate our careers more effectively in the new world of work.

I am privileged to mentor young South Africans as they seek to effectively navigate their careers. I am humbled by the challenges they face, including carrying the financial burdens of less fortunate families and the immense pressure to succeed in the corporate world. I am grateful to each of you for sharing your views and thoughts with me and allowing me to learn from your experiences. A special thank you to Noma Zwane and Zanele Phungwayo who have inspired me and other South Africans to become more.

Thank you to the mentors and coaches who have worked alongside me. A special thank you to Ruth Jackson, Cherene Blues, Lynette Lemmer and Marina Gunter who have tirelessly supported me in all my efforts. A word of thanks to WP whose social media ideas are always welcome.

Thank you to Penguin for agreeing to publish this book and to Reneé Naudé for assisting us to produce the final manuscript. It has been a pleasure working with you on this book.

May this book inspire you to see what may be possible for you and assist you to make it a reality.

Johannesburg
April 2012

Graeme:

A year ago I received a request out of the blue: 'I want to write a book. Would you please contribute and write it with me?' With Kerry based in Johannesburg and me in London, it took some time before we were able to meet and chat through the project. But during that time, I got to know of Kerry's work over many years helping people to make meaningful career decisions and guiding them into their dream jobs. I learnt about the model of career navigation she's been perfecting during that time. There seemed to be something special about her approach and her results were certainly impressive.

My interest has always been in the changing world of work as I research, present and consult to organisations all around the world together with my team at my company, TomorrowToday. Kerry's request required me to look at the work world with different eyes. And so I welcomed the opportunity to move from a more strategic and conceptual level, where I normally do most of my work, to a much more practical, tangible and personal level.

And so began our collaboration. I was happy to provide insights into the new world of work, and how this might impact the way in which people should go about shaping their careers. I know that this book will support Kerry's goal of seeing more and more people find lifelong job satisfaction and personal fulfilment.

My own career navigation story would have been a good case study for this book. I feel incredibly privileged that before I turned 30 I had stumbled across some of the secrets we present in the following pages. I feel that I get to live out my dream every day, and have a job and lifestyle that is almost perfect for me. If we can help even just a few people to achieve the same for themselves, the effort in writing this book will have been worth it.

During the writing of this book, TomorrowToday, celebrated its tenth anniversary. We're a small company, based across three continents, drawn together by our passion to see a new way of working emerge. I want to thank my team for their support and encouragement, and for their examples of how to make great career decisions and live with the consequences. I also want to thank all of the people who have worked with, and for me over the years. Each one has contributed in some way to shaping my life today. It's always dangerous to highlight individuals when there are so many who deserves thanks, but I want to especially thank Lynda Smith (for her wisdom, support and example of indefatigable work that benefits and uplifts others), Keith Coats (for his quiet, deliberate focus and demands for quality and significance) and Nikki Bush (for proving that it is possible to do it all).

I would also like to thank the many friends in my life who are living out their dreams, or at least navigating their careers towards that goal, and whose lives are an inspiration to me as they do so. Once again, a few special mentions from a list that could fill many pages: Craig and Helen Pournara, David and Nikki Lock, Jeremy and Sue Farrell, Terry and Nikki Bakker, Graeme and Regan Berry, Barrie Bramley, Michael Mol, Pete Laburn, Pete and Charlene Schumacher, Jono and Kayleen Clarke-Howard, Damon and Lauren Foster, Paul Bridle, John Cremer, Grant Driver, Helen Nicolson, Justin Cohen, Jules Newton, Buhle Dlamini, Brian Helsby, W Mitchell, Matt Crabtree, Lesley Everett, Gary

Bailey, Wayne and Raylene Shipham, Dave and Sue Shipster, Brian and Shirley Douglas, Nick and Trish Bekker, Noiy and Bronwyn Prommathat, Colin and Grietjie Phelps, Brian McLaren and John Benn. Thank you to all of you, and many, many others just like you who create an environment around me that is so healthy and inspiring.

As I reflect on these acknowledgements, it's interesting to me that many of my family members have also recently made important and inspirational career navigation moves. I thank them, too, for the way in which their lives continue to shape mine, including: my wife Jane (studying again in preparation for the time when her focus can shift from our own children to the children of others), my father Reg (building a new university in the Natal Midlands), my mother Ruth (building a new life in Pretoria), my in-laws Paul and Eunice (not quite managing to retire and do nothing in Cape Town), my brother (chasing his dream career in America), my sister (putting in the hard yards to build her dream career), my brother-in-law Tony (risking it all to build something that's his own, and then landing an Olympic contract in his first year), and a plethora of aunts, uncles and cousins all demonstrating the glorious diversity of the career choices available in the wonderful world of possibility we now inhabit. Thank you to my family for your examples, and your support.

And then, finally, thanks to the team that has made this particular book possible. Thanks to the tireless editors, designers and professionals at Penguin SA, headed by Reneé Naudé, who have beaten and massaged this book into shape. Thanks again for making the task of writing and publishing a book just that little less difficult than it could be.

My wish for you as you read this book is that it would inspire and equip you to find career success, and navigate the turbulent but rewarding waters of a new world of work.

Wimbledon, London
April 2012